LEADING WELL AT HOME

How Husbands and Fathers Can Biblically Lead Their Families

ERIC RUTHERFORD

Entrusting the Faith

www.entrustingthefaith.com

Leading Well at Home: How Husbands and Fathers Can Biblically Lead Their Families

Copyright © 2020 by Eric Rutherford

Published by Entrusting the Faith
        P.O. Box 10452
        Murfreesboro, TN 37129
        www.entrustingthefaith.com

Published in association with Entrusting The Faith, www.entrustingthefaith.com

Front image copyright © 2020 JRR Designs
Cover design copyright © 2020 JRR Designs

Published 2020
Printed in the United States of America

ISBN: 978-1-7350821-0-3
Ebook ISBN: 978-1-7350821-1-0

To Rachel,
my beloved bride and
precious gift from the Lord

CONTENTS

Introduction

Taking a break from painting our kitchen to help my wife prepare dinner, I put away the paint, brushes and rollers, then moved my step-ladder into the corner. While we were cooking, I looked around for my son, trying to make sure he was not getting into anything—he was two after all. I found him in the corner of the room, standing two rungs from the top of the stepladder. In that moment, I did not shout or raise my voice. In fact, I did not say anything at all. Instead, I quickly walked over to him, lifted him from the ladder, and eased him back down to the floor. After redirecting his attention elsewhere, I moved the ladder into the garage until I needed it again.

I learned three important lessons through that experience.

1. It is very easy for people—myself included—to put themselves unknowingly into a dangerous situation. My son had no trouble climbing the ladder, but I do not know if he could have climbed back down. Like most children, he was just doing what he wanted to do, but there probably would have been negative repercussions if I had not interceded.

2. Problems are resolved by taking action. Telling my son to climb down the ladder might have been fine, but I doubt he could have actually climbed down safely. This situation required my intervention.

3. We mimic what we see. He probably climbed the ladder because he saw me do it. We learn how to do things by trying what we see someone else do—this is just how we learn because that is how God designed us.

Just like my son learned how to climb a ladder by watching me, my children will learn what it means to be a husband and a father from me. I will be their greatest influence for good or for ill. If the Lord allows my son to marry and have children, I will be the first influence on what he believes it looks like to be a husband and a father. What we talk about, what I teach him, what he sees me do, how I interact with my wife, how I pursue the Lord—all of this will impact him. If the Lord allows my two daughters to marry and have children, I will be their first influence on how they believe a husband ought to treat his wife and children. How I reflect Christ in my words and actions, how I serve my wife and my children, how I work both in and out of the home—all of this and more will impact them deeply.

I feel the weight of this every day, but I do not want it to be different. I also know that I am not alone. If you are a husband and/or a father, you probably feel this weight too.

THE IMPORTANCE OF CLEAR AND ACCURATE INSTRUCTIONS

I can hear you now. "Eric," you will say to me, "I read the Bible and believe what it says. I want to lead my family well, but I need help understanding what to *do*." My response is to say, "Yes, we need help. I definitely need it, too."

I have found that systematic instructions are important. Sometimes, in my arrogance, I don't think I need them, but I have to confess that things go better when I follow them. You may feel the same way too. For example, I just purchased a bracket to hang my television on the wall of our living room. I know the concept of how to hang it: find the studs, drill holes into the studs for the bracket, attach the bracket to the television, and hang the television. When I brought the bracket home, however, I did not pull the pieces out and just go for it. (I know some of you could do it, but I am not that savvy.) Instead, I read the instructions to make sure I understood the details of what was needed and how to make it work with this particular bracket and television. Then, I found the appropriate tools and started to work with instructions in-hand.

There is a problem though—sometimes the instructions do not help. My son likes to play with building blocks. Over the years, I have helped him put many sets together. I have discovered that not all instruction manuals are created equal. Several manufacturers make such blocks. I will not mention specific brand names, but one company does a great job with clear instructions and helpful pictures. Their directions are easy to follow and just make sense. Another company does not do so well. The illustrations are decent, but it's not always clear how things fit. Without fail, when we work on one of these sets, we have to disassemble and reassemble portions of it. I always cringe when I see this brand.

As we travel through the chapters of this book together, you will notice the thoughts and applications I provide are based on the Word of God—that is not an accident. Scripture needs to be the basis for our lives. Looking at the world as our instruction manual for what it means to be a husband and a father is like looking at the instructions of the second building block company—it does not go well. Instead, we need to reach for God's Word as our source for instruction.

A SANCTIFICATION COMPANION

As a follower of Christ, from the moment we trust in Him, we start the road of sanctification. This is the process of becoming more like Christ and less like sin. This journey will not cease until we die or the Lord returns. Each day we are at war with our sinful nature. We desperately need the Holy Spirit to strengthen us and help us take every thought captive to obey Christ (2 Corinthians 10:5). Sanctification is a process, and so is learning how to serve your family as a husband and father.

Think of this book as a sanctification companion—a basic list of action items that can help you biblically lead your families well. While other books and resources take a deep-dive into the facets of what it means to be a good husband and father, this book is more like a launching pad. It will provide ideas to help you take the next right step, and the next right step after that, and the next right step after that. We will ask some tough questions, but—and this is the key—**the goal is to get you farther in your walk with the Lord and your relationships with your wife and your children than you are today.**

A quick warning—if you think I am a perfect person who has never made mistakes, then you will be greatly disappointed. I have failed hard and frequently, and I am not proud of the way I have caused my wife grief and sorrow, or the ways I have disappointed my children. The Lord has not only redeemed me, but He has redeemed my marriage and my family. This is all because of His grace and my willingness to submit to Him and His Word.

In light of my mistakes and His grace, this is the book I wish I could have read at the beginning of my marriage—not only to read it, but to apply it and go through it together with other like-minded men so that we could better serve Christ and our families. I do not want you to experience my failures and I do not want your wives to go through the sorrow that my wife has faced. Instead, I want you to be aware of the trials and snares that exist in the life of a husband and father so that you can avoid them.

Ah, but this is not simply a book about things to avoid. It is also a resource filled with actions to take and examples to follow. My story does not end with my failures, but has grown through the working of the Holy Spirit in my life so that I can lead well at home. Just like you, I do not lead perfectly. I continue to learn and grow. I am farther along the path than I was three years ago, but I am continually pursuing Christ so that three years from now I will be even farther along the path than I am today. I am a not-yet-finished product—and so are you. Today, you too stand somewhere along that path as an imperfect, work-in-progress husband or father. Make the decision that three years from now you will be farther along the path than you are today.

LET'S DO THIS!

Remember, you are not alone—we are in this together. Let's walk through this book together, identifying specific action steps as we go. Build on what I have learned so that your families will pursue Christ with their whole hearts because you—their husband and father—do too.

As you read through this book:

- Grab a pen and a notebook.
- Write down thoughts and ideas you want to remember.
- Record specific, measurable goals.
- Take intentional steps to reach those goals.
- Gather a group of like-minded men together and talk through this book with them, encouraging one another and stirring up one another to love and good works (Hebrews 10:24).

I will provide a list of "quick hits" at the end of each chapter that summarize key ideas, along with a few questions for reflection. These questions will prompt you to answer with actionable steps based on how the Lord directs you during that chapter. At the end of the book, I have provided a more in-depth small group study guide for each chapter which you can use either on your own or together with a group of men.

Remember, this is a book of action, not simply words of encouragement. So if you are ready, let's begin!

QUICK HITS FROM THE INTRODUCTION

- We will be the greatest influence on our families for good or ill.
- Our children will learn what a husband and father looks like by watching and listening to us.
- We cannot provide salvation for our wife or our children—only Christ can do that. However, how we value Christ will directly affect their view of Christ.

QUESTIONS FOR REFLECTION

1. How has your father's influence affected the way you see your role as a husband or a father?
2. What do you want out of this book?
3. List one step you can take in order to apply what you have learned in the introduction.

CHAPTER 1

Where Do We Start?

How do we begin this journey toward being a spirit-led father and husband? When in doubt, start with the basics and the fundamentals. Just like when you learn how to play an instrument or a sport, it is crucial to start at the beginning and learn the foundational skills. So let's begin with the basics of being a Christian and work our way through what Scripture specifically teaches us about being a godly man, husband, and father.

WHAT DOES IT MEAN TO BE A FOLLOWER OF CHRIST?

To be a follower of Christ means we believe that Jesus Christ:

- was who He said He was (the Son of God, the Promised One from the Old Testament) and who the Bible says He is (specifically God)
- was born to a virgin through the power of the Holy Spirit
- lived a sinless life
- allowed Himself to be killed on the cross for our sins
- was buried

- was resurrected
- appeared to over five hundred people after His resurrection
- ascended into heaven
- will one day return.

To be a follower of Christ is to acknowledge that I:

- am a sinner with no hope and no way of fixing my sin against God on my own.
- ask forgiveness from Christ for my sin and believe that He forgives all who seek it.
- look ahead to an eternity in His presence as I strive to grow in holiness while on this earth.
- seek to know Him, not in an academic or informational way, but in a relationship.
- submit to the Lord, trusting not in myself, but in His work through Christ.

WHAT DOES THE BIBLE SAY TO HUSBANDS AND FATHERS?

If we are followers of Christ, we need to ask, "What is Jesus telling me I need to do?" It is simple enough in concept, but immensely challenging in practice.

In Matthew, Jesus is asked what is the greatest commandment, and he answers the lawyer of the Pharisees with this statement: "You shall love the Lord your God with all your heart and with all your soul and with all your mind. This is the great and first commandment. And a second is like it: You shall love your neighbor as yourself. On these two commandments depend

all the Law and the Prophets" (Matthew 22:37-40). This is
the essence of following Christ: **love God and love people.**
However, this is not a fluffy stuffed animal and chocolates kind
of Valentine's Day love. It is not a feeling, but an action. To love
is to act. To love is to do.

The Bible provides great insight into how to be a husband and
father. Sometimes it has very clear "do this, do not do that"
phrases and sometimes it provides some specific examples of
"do this, but do not do this under any circumstances." Let's start
with being a husband.

WHAT TO DO AS A HUSBAND

As a husband, I need to realize my job is not to be the "boss" but
to be a servant to my family. In Ephesians 5, Paul gives a superb
example of how we are to serve our families with three very
clear commands for husbands:

> "Husbands, love your wives, as Christ loved the church
> and gave himself up for her" (Ephesians 5:25).

> "In the same way husbands should love their wives as
> their own bodies. He who loves his wife loves himself.
> For no one ever hated his own flesh, but nourishes
> and cherishes it, just as Christ does the church"
> (Ephesians 5:28-29).

> "However, let each one of you love his wife as himself"
> (Ephesians 5:33a).

To love as Christ loved the church is to love sacrificially and
to be obedient to God. It is to submit to God fully. I know you
might be thinking, "That's great Eric, but what does it look like

17

in real life? What do I *do*?" I am glad you asked! Jesus models this sacrificial love for us, so we can look to Him. We read in Philippians about Christ's sacrifice by coming here to earth, where Paul writes,

> Have this mind among yourselves, which is yours in Christ Jesus, who, though he was in the form of God, did not count equality with God a thing to be grasped, but emptied himself, by taking the form of a servant, being born in the likeness of men. And being found in human form, he humbled himself by becoming obedient to the point of death, even death on a cross (Philippians 2:5-8).

Selfish pride has no place in the life of a husband. If Christ humbled Himself and was obedient to the Father, leaving heaven for earth to be a servant, then we who follow Him are to do likewise.

I am to love my wife by serving her and nurturing holiness in her walk with the Lord. To love my wife as my own body is to put her needs first, knowing that by doing so I am serving Christ and serving her. To love my wife as I love myself is to make sure I am concerned for her well-being and to give as much attention to her as I would to myself.

What does this look like in everyday life? Watching the kids so she can have a few quiet minutes alone with God, praying for and with her everyday, or even by selflessly helping out with the chores are all practical examples. Do not make it too complicated and when in doubt, ask her. Tell her you want to learn how to serve her better and ask her how you can do this.

WHAT NOT TO DO AS A HUSBAND

One of the many beautiful things about the Bible is how it does not paint God's people as perfect. It is an encouragement and a humble reminder that if they could not do it perfectly on their own, then I will not live perfectly apart from Christ either.

We see several instances throughout the Old Testament of men who did not always love their wives as Christ loved the Church. Some of these men are considered heroes of the faith and lived extraordinarily faithful lives to the Lord; however, even they sinned and fell short. This is not a license to sin, but a stark reminder that we are all one step away from a fall.

We can look back in Genesis 2 and 3 at how Adam acts and see many similarities to how we act. First, the Lord gave Adam the commandment not to eat of the Tree of Knowledge of Good and Evil, and he was responsible to communicate this to Eve (Genesis 2:15-17). Second, Adam stood by doing nothing while the Serpent persuaded Eve to eat the fruit. She then ate the fruit and Adam ate it too (Genesis 3:1-6). Third, Adam blamed God when it was his own sinful actions which led him into trouble and separated him from God. "The woman whom you gave to be with me, she gave me fruit of the tree, and I ate" (Genesis 3:12).

The Lord has given us His Word, and we are to learn it, teach it, and be obedient to it. It is easy for us to just sit back and let things happen, as Adam did. Instead of standing firm and protecting our families from the deception of Satan, we can go along with it. When things go wrong, we blame everyone but ourselves. I wish I could say I have not done this, but unfortunately, I have. Adam did not protect Eve and stand between her and Satan, instead he agreed to act sinfully along with Eve (Genesis 3). We, as husbands, need to be watchful and ready to defend our families against sinful enemies. Do not stand idly as an observer. The consequences for inaction can be catastrophic (as Adam found out).

A little later in Genesis, we see Abraham claim Sarah as his sister instead of his wife because he feared that the Egyptians would kill him in order to take Sarah (Genesis 12). He did likewise in Genesis 20 when they entered the land of Gerar and met Abimelech the king. Isaac, Abraham's son, follows this example in Genesis 26 and repeats Abraham's folly in Gerar, claiming Rebekah as his sister instead of acknowledging her as his wife. Isaac then ignored God's promise to Rebekah in Genesis 25, when the Lord told Rebekah about her two sons how "the older shall serve the younger" (Genesis 25:23).

Two quick takeaways: first, do not be ashamed or afraid to tell the world that the woman beside you is your wife. The Lord purposely gave her to you. She is a gift and a treasure—be proud of her! The second takeaway is that the Lord speaks to her like He speaks to you. Listen to her and seek her counsel—God gave her to you. I have learned the hard way that my wife and I need to be in agreement on major decisions, and if we are not, then I need to pray and ask the Lord to either change her mind or change *my* mind. In chapter two you will read about some of my foolish actions which could have been avoided if I had followed this advice. Remember, leading well does not mean we have all of the answers or we only do things our way. The Lord gave us our wives so we would work together.

Jacob was a treasure trove of poor choices with women. He loved Rachel, but was tricked by her father Laban into marrying Leah, her older sister (Genesis 29). Jacob then made an arrangement with Laban to marry Rachel too. The sinful pattern of having more than one wife began back in Genesis 4:19

with Lamech. Lamech took two wives and anytime this pattern occured, bad things followed because it goes against God's design of marriage as denoted in Genesis 2 and elsewhere in Scripture.

David also married more than one wife and ultimately arranged for the death of Uriah the Hittie so he could marry Uriah's wife, Bathsheba (2 Samuel 11). The result of this sin is tragedy for David, his family, and the land of Israel as God brought judgment upon him. Remember, the Lord gave us our wives, knowing even before He set the stars in the sky that we would be married to this woman today.

Please, do not let your eyes wander the way David's did, but instead keep your eyes on your bride. Avoid movies, websites, restaurants, sports, or any other situation where women are not modestly dressed. Delight yourself in your wife by saying something positive or admirable about her each day. Disastrous results will ensue if we fail at this—as evidenced by these biblical characters.

In these instances, these men did not serve their wives consistently, but put their own desires, feelings, and patterns of the world ahead of obedience to God.

We don't get the full narrative of many of these stories, so we can't hear all of the words spoken between husband and wife. But our words can do amazing things: build up, tear down, spur to great heights, and defeat the best intentions. As husbands, we need to build up, encourage and support our wives always. "Husbands, love your wives, and do not be harsh with them" (Colossians 3:19).

When a husband says anything negative about his wife in public and tries to pass it off as a joke, I instantly imagine how hurt his wife would feel if she heard his words. It is a passive-aggressive act that demeans the very person who has committed to spend her life with him. Speaking such things about your wife in public doesn't make you look better. It says to every person in the room, "My wife is an idiot and let me tell you how."

Take a closer look at your words and evaluate whether this is you. And if it is, let's pause for just a moment, take a deep breath, and remember there is hope. Christ can redeem all things, and He certainly continues to redeem my mistakes and my sin.

Start by praying to the Lord, asking for forgiveness, repenting (turning from this behavior), and asking Him to help you break this pattern. Second, go to your wife, ask her for forgiveness, and tell her about your heart change. By acknowledging our sin to our wives in situations like these, it shows her we recognize our sinful actions *and* we are correcting the behavior. This is not an act of weakness, but an act of humility that will strengthen our marriages. Continue praying each day that the Lord will help you restrain from saying any words that are harmful or damaging to her. Share this commitment with a few Christian men you trust, and ask them to pray for you and to keep you accountable. Lastly, praise your wife during conversations with other people, especially when she is present.

WHAT TO DO AS A DAD

What do we need to do specifically as a dad? Let's look at a few examples.

"Fathers, do not provoke your children to anger, but bring them up in the discipline and instruction of the Lord" (Ephesians 6:4).

We need to lead our children in such a way that they see Christ in us as we lead them towards Christ. I have done some bone-headed stuff with my children—and I bet you have too. I have lost my temper when they acted like children (which they were) or when they did not respond as I wanted them to. The times where I have felt the worst are when we have arrived at church on Sunday morning and I have needed to pause before we get out of our minivan to ask my children to forgive me for what I have said in anger. I am convinced the Lord gives us children as a daily reminder of how much we need His grace.

When Joshua was preparing the people of Israel before they crossed the Jordan River into the Promised Land, he had them set up twelve stones on the eastern border of Jericho at Gilgal. He then told the people,

> When your children ask their fathers in times to come, "What do these stones mean?" then you shall let your children know, "Israel passed over this Jordan on dry ground." For the Lord your God dried up the waters of the Jordan for you until you passed over, as the Lord your God did to the Red Sea, which he dried up for us until we passed over, so that all the peoples of the earth may know that the hand of the Lord is mighty, that you may fear the Lord your God forever (Joshua 4:21-24).

Joshua told the people to tell their children about the Lord and how He delivered them from Egypt. He gave them a physical reminder (the twelve stones) as a way to point their children to God's grace. Though we do not have those stones, we can use other examples throughout the day and week to tell our children about the Lord and His grace. We should talk with our kids about how the Lord is working in us and around us. We can direct our thanksgiving to the Lord for the food, clothing, and home which

He has provided. We should thank the Lord for the very breath we breathe because it is all an act of His mercy and grace toward us. Let our children hear these things come from our mouths and see us act with thanksgiving.

Another example is found at the beginning of Psalm 78:1-8. The psalmist writes,

> Give ear, O my people, to my teaching;
>   incline your ears to the words of my mouth!
> I will open my mouth in a parable;
>   I will utter dark sayings from of old,
> things that we have heard and known,
>   that our fathers have told us.
> We will not hide them from their children,
>   but tell to the coming generation
> the glorious deeds of the Lord, and his might,
>   and the wonders that he has done.
>
> He established a testimony in Jacob
>   and appointed a law in Israel,
> which he commanded our fathers
>   to teach to their children,
> that the next generation might know them,
>   the children yet unborn,
> and arise and tell them to their children,
>   so that they should set their hope in God
> and not forget the works of God,
>   but keep his commandments;
> and that they should not be like their fathers,
>   a stubborn and rebellious generation,
> a generation whose heart was not steadfast,
>   whose spirit was not faithful to God.

The psalmist guides us through the example of hearing what our fathers and elders have taught regarding the Lord and then doing the same thing for our children. He then points out how the Lord commanded it so the future generations would set their hope on the Lord unlike the previous generations who turned from the Lord and went their own way. We will not remember unless someone teaches us, so let's teach our children. And we will not maintain our allegiance to the Lord unless we consistently remind one another, so let's invite our children to remind us where our loyalties lie.

If you did not grow up in a home where someone taught you about Jesus, it is okay. You can still begin a legacy with your own family and establish the foundation for them. It is not about where you start, but that you start. In chapter seven, we will go through several ways that we as fathers can lead our children spiritually, but one place you can start right now is to sit down with your children and say, "I love you and I want you to know about Jesus. I know I am responsible for teaching you about Him and showing you how to follow Him. I did not not have an example growing up, but I want to learn how to be one for you. Please pray for me as I learn how to do this."

If you have never talked with your children about Christ, taking this step will drastically change your relationship with them for the better. It may feel weird or absolutely terrifying (trust me, I know), but they will see a man who is humbling himself before Christ with a teachable heart. You will model for them how it is okay and appropriate to take that posture before Jesus.

Remember, the goal is to be farther along the path next year than you are today, and to be farther along the path in five years than you are next year. This step will lead you a bit farther along that path.

Paul writes in Colossians, "Fathers, do not provoke your children, lest they become discouraged" (Colossians 3:21). He tells us not to let our anger, attitudes, and actions be an impediment to our child's pursuit of Christ. Even if we represent Christ well, our children may reject Him, so do not let our sinful actions discourage them from pursuing Christ.

The Lord lays out very challenging and convicting words in Exodus 20:4-6:

> You shall not make for yourself a carved image, or any likeness of anything that is in heaven above, or that is in the earth beneath, or that is in the water under the earth. You shall not bow down to them or serve them, for I the Lord your God am a jealous God, visiting the iniquity of the fathers on the children to the third and the fourth generation of those who hate me, but showing steadfast love to thousands of those who love me and keep my commandments.

There are two very different results based on how we live and what we do. If we love the Lord and pursue Him, our faith will affect those who come after us—like our children and grandchildren—through the working of the Holy Spirit. If we reject the Lord and bow down to idols and idolatry, there are consequences for our families—not just our children, but generations to come. This does not mean that our faith in Christ will save our children or future generations, but our faith will guide them toward the path of righteousness in Christ.

WHAT NOT TO DO AS A DAD

Some not so good examples of how fathers cared for (and didn't care for) their children exist in the Bible as well. Let's start with Isaac. Back in Genesis 25:28 we see that Isaac loved Esau, his first born. Isaac's wife Rebekah loved Jacob, Easu's brother, but we do not see the same fondness between Isaac and Jacob.

In Genesis 27, Isaac wants to give his blessing to Esau before he dies. Normally, this would be fine because Esau is the oldest and the blessing would naturally fall to him due to birth order. The problem is God had told Rebekah something quite different before Jacob and Esau were born. "And the Lord said to her, 'Two nations are in your womb, and two peoples from within you shall be divided; the one shall be stronger than the other, the older shall serve the younger'" (Genesis 25:23). Isaac rejected this logic and was preparing to bless Esau because he was partial to Esau's food—essentially, Isaac favored Esau.

As Genesis 27 plays out, we see that Jacob deceived Isaac and gained the blessing instead of Esau. He then fled so that Esau would not kill him. The consequence for Isaac's favoritism of one son over the other and his disobedience to God led to the separation of his family and he passed on his sinful attitudes to his children.

Jacob repeated the very same pattern with his children. "Now Israel [Jacob] loved Joseph more than any other of his sons, because he was the son of his old age. And he made him a robe of many colors. But when his brothers saw that their father loved him more than all his brothers, they hated him and could not speak peacefully to him" (Genesis 37:3-4). This jealousy led his brothers to sell Joseph into slavery. Jacob played favorites not only with his wives (he favored Rachel over Leah), but also with his children (Joseph was Rachel's first son).

Isaac displayed the same type of favoritism with his sons, so it is not a surprise that Jacob did this too. Remember, our children watch us and therefore do what we do. My son climbed a ladder when he was two because I climbed a ladder.

In Genesis 42, the brothers went down to Egypt to get grain because of a famine and unknowingly spoke with Joseph, who was now the second most powerful person in Egypt, second only to Pharaoh. Joseph told them to not come back without Benjamin, who was Joseph's full brother (the only other son of Jacob and Rachel). When the brothers arrived home and told Jacob about all that happened, Jacob responded, "My son shall not go down with you, for his brother is dead, and he is the only one left. If harm should happen to him on the journey that you are to make, you would bring down my gray hairs with sorrow to Sheol" (Genesis 42:38).

Think about what Jacob said and to whom he said it: Benjamin (my son) will not go because his brother (Joseph) is dead and he (Benjamin) is all that is left. Jacob said this to nine of his sons (Simeon was stuck in Egypt). He essentially told them, "I have two sons. You do not count."

The Lord worked through these two situations to achieve His purposes, but Isaac's and Jacob's sinful actions caused significant problems which rippled throughout history. Aren't you glad we can learn from scripture instead of living a story like this in our own life? My children desperately want to know they are loved and accepted by me—their dad—and I desperately want them to know I love and accept them because of who they are, *not because of what they do or how successful they become.*

HOW DOES THIS RELATE TO RESPONSIBILITY AND ACCOUNTABILITY?

Think with me for a minute about responsibility and let's define responsibility and accountability. An example that comes to mind is the manager of a large retail store like Walmart or Lowe's. The manager does not do all of the work in the store. He does not unload every truck that delivers to the loading dock nor does he stock all of the shelves. He does not check out every customer who goes through the checkout line or handle every person who goes to the customer service desk. He does not bring every cart from the parking lot back into the store or empty every trashcan or sweep every floor. He does not make every decision on inventory or personnel scheduling.

He does work in the store and may help with any and all of the tasks, but the difference is if anything goes wrong within the store, the manager is ultimately responsible and will be held accountable. His name and phone number are listed on a wall inside of the building for any questions or problems customers may have. In a similar way, President Harry Truman had a sign on his desk in the Oval Office that said, "The buck stops here," meaning he would not pass the responsibility to anyone else—he was ultimately accountable for what happened while he was President. In the same way, we are responsible and held accountable for our own families.

Jesus explains this further in the following parable in Matthew 25:14-29:

> For it will be like a man going on a journey, who called his servants and entrusted to them his property. To one he gave five talents, to another two, to another one, to each according to his ability. Then he went away.

He who had received the five talents went at once and traded with them, and he made five talents more. So also he who had the two talents made two talents more. But he who had received the one talent went and dug in the ground and hid his master's money. Now after a long time the master of those servants came and settled accounts with them. And he who had received the five talents came forward, bringing five talents more, saying, "Master, you delivered to me five talents; here, I have made five talents more." His master said to him, "Well done, good and faithful servant. You have been faithful over a little; I will set you over much. Enter into the joy of your master." And he also who had the two talents came forward, saying, "Master, you delivered to me two talents; here, I have made two talents more." His master said to him, "Well done, good and faithful servant. You have been faithful over a little; I will set you over much. Enter into the joy of your master." He also who had received the one talent came forward, saying, "Master, I knew you to be a hard man, reaping where you did not sow, and gathering where you scattered no seed, so I was afraid, and I went and hid your talent in the ground. Here, you have what is yours." But his master answered him, "You wicked and slothful servant! You knew that I reap where I have not sown and gather where I scattered no seed? Then you ought to have invested my money with the bankers, and at my coming I should have received what was my own with interest. So take the talent from him and give it to him who has the ten talents. For to everyone who has will more be given, and he will have an abundance. But from the one who has not, even what he has will be taken away. And cast the worthless servant into the outer darkness. In that place there will be weeping and gnashing of teeth.

Like the servants, the Lord gives us talents and puts things into our care. Some of those things are the spiritual gifts we receive from the Holy Spirit when we first put our faith in Christ. The Lord gives us different skills, abilities, and interests outside of spiritual gifts for us to use, develop, and apply in our lives as well. He also asks us to be responsible for our wife and children. As a husband and father, this sobering parable weighs heavily on me. I know that I am not responsible for my children's salvation, nor my wife's. However, the Lord has entrusted them to me and I am responsible to make wise decisions and model Christ-likeness for them, teaching and leading according to His Word by the power of His Spirit. I will stand before the Lord one day and give an account, just like the servants did in the parable, and the Lord will ask me what I did with what He entrusted to me. You will have the same opportunity before the Lord, too.

As a husband and father, responsibility and accountability do not mean I have to do everything, be involved in everything, or make all the decisions. That is not healthy, nor is it biblical. It does mean, however, I have an intentional role to play. So, how do I start taking responsibility or check to make sure I am handling responsibility well? We will answer those questions in the next few chapters.

QUICK HITS FROM THE CHAPTER

- As husbands, we are called to love and serve our wives and children.
- The Bible gives us many examples of how to do this well.
- Scripture also shows us several examples of men who did not love and serve their families well, like Isaac and Jacob.
- We are responsible for our families and will be held accountable for what we do with all the Lord has given to us.

QUESTIONS FOR REFLECTION

1. Are you a follower of Christ? On what are you basing your answer?
2. How has your view changed on what the Bible describes as the role of a husband and father?
3. What action is God asking you to take based on this chapter?
4. What kind of legacy do you want to leave?
5. What things do you want your children to learn from you (either by observing you or by being taught from you)?

CHAPTER 2

How to Start

One of the great things about the Bible is it is understandable. The Lord spoke through the biblical writers in a way their audience could understand—and that includes us.

WHAT KIND OF FRUIT ARE YOU PRODUCING?

One of the examples used repeatedly is sowing and reaping. Sowing and reaping is not upper level calculus or organic chemistry difficult. In fact, you and I can describe it quite easily and know exactly how it works because it is something as obvious to us as gravity. If you do not believe me, let's try it right now. I will ask you a question and you fill in the answer.

Question #1: An apple comes from what kind of tree?

Okay, one more question and I will phrase it differently.

Question #2: What fruit would I pick from an orange tree?

Now we need to check our answers. Did you say an *apple* comes from an apple tree? Excellent! Did you say you would find an *orange* on an orange tree? Great! Two for two!

Why did you not answer *banana* for the fruit that comes from an apple tree? Why didn't you say you would pick *peaches* from an orange tree? The answer is because apple seeds grow into apple trees that bear apples, and orange seeds grow into orange trees that bear oranges. What you plant is what you get.

If you ever get the chance to watch the movie *Second-Hand Lions*,[1] please do so. It is a delightful movie on so many levels. The basic premise is that a boy named Walter goes to live with his two great uncles, Hub and Garth. Walter tries to help his uncles in several different ways. At one point, Hub and Garth buy seeds from a traveling salesman and plant a big garden with one row designated for each kind of seed they purchased. As the plants started to grow, Walter asked which plant was in a particular row, so Garth answered based on the sign at the beginning of the row. Walter asked the same question about a different row and Garth answered based on a different sign. As they started looking around, they noticed all of the plants looked alike—they were all corn—but only one seed packet was labeled corn. At this point, they realized the salesperson tricked them. You see, the fact that the seed packet said "beets" or "peas" did not make any difference because the seed itself was corn. Corn seed produces corn every time, even if you want beans.

Paul writes in Galatians 6:7-8, "Do not be deceived: God is not mocked for whatever one sows, that he will also reap. For the one who sows to his own flesh will from the flesh reap corruption, but the one who sows to the Spirit will from the Spirit reap eternal life." In this instance, Paul describes the difference between faith in Christ and faith in self with two very different results based on what was sown. You cannot plant one thing and get something else.

Another example of sowing occurs in Matthew 13:24-30, where Jesus tells the following parable.

> The kingdom of heaven may be compared to a man who sowed good seed in his field, but while his men were sleeping, his enemy came and sowed weeds among the wheat and went away. So when the plants came up and bore grain, then the weeds appeared also. And the servants of the master of the house came and said to him, "Master, did you not sow good seed in your field? How then does it have weeds?" He said to them, "An enemy has done this." So the servants said to him, "Then do you want us to go and gather them?" But he said, "No, lest in gathering the weeds you root up the wheat along with them. Let both grow together until the harvest, and at harvest time I will tell the reapers, 'Gather the weeds first and bind them in bundles to be burned, but gather the wheat into my barn.'"

In this parable, there is a clear distinction between the wheat and the weeds beginning with the seeds planted. When the plants matured, the wheat seeds grew into wheat and the weed seeds grew into weeds—there was no doubt which was good and which was not. The results at harvest time were clear too: wheat was valued and gathered into the barn while the weeds were removed and burned. This is a stark yet decidedly clear example.

If I say I am a follower of Christ and saved by faith in Him alone, that can be completely true. I can be sealed by the Holy Spirit (Ephesians 1:13), saved by grace through faith (Ephesians 2:8), be a child and heir of the King (Romans 8:16-17), and yet some fruit in my life may resemble something else because I am sowing the wrong seeds. What I mentally acknowledge as true about Jesus and my allegiance to Him, and how I physically order my life may not be in complete alignment. Let's look at three places in our lives where this might be true: how we use our time, how we spend our money, and what interests receive our attention.

HOW WE USE OUR TIME

The beauty and tragedy of time is that we all have the same amount each day. If the Lord allows both of us to live for the next week, we will each have 168 hours to use. We cannot increase the number of hours or minutes we possess in the next week or borrow against a future date or save them for a later week. If the Lord is willing, at the end of the next seven days, you and I will have lived 168 hours.

Let's take this out further. If the Lord is willing and we live for the next five years, we will have 1,825 days (I am ignoring leap years in this exercise) or 43,800 hours. We will have 1,825 days (or 43,800 hours) to spend at work or play, with family or away from family, seeking the Lord or ignoring Him.

How about one more. If the Lord were to grant us a life of eighty years birth-to-death, we would have 29,200 days or 700,800 hours on this earth. This is all the time we will have to influence the people around us for good or for ill, for Christ or for self. 29,200 days sounds like a huge amount of time, but let's put this into a real-life scenario and use me as the example.

If the Lord lets me live to my eightieth birthday and the Lord lets my wife live to my eightieth birthday, my life can be divided accordingly. (For the sake of simplicity with the following numbers, I will assume that both of our birthdays are January 1, that each child goes to college on August 8, and there are no leap years).

PERIODS OF LIFE	DAY #	# OF DAYS	% OF LIFE
TOTAL DAYS OF LIFE	**1-29,200**	**29,200**	**100.00%**
TOTAL DAYS BEFORE MARRIAGE	**1-9440**	**9440**	**32.31%**
TOTAL DAYS MARRIED	**9440-29,200**	**19,780**	**67.69%**
TOTAL DAYS 1ST CHILD AT HOME	**11,688-18,482**	**6794**	**23.25%**
TOTAL DAYS 2ND CHILD AT HOME	**12,053-18,847**	**6794**	**23.25%**
TOTAL DAYS 3RD CHILD AT HOME	**13,149-19,943**	**6794**	**23.25%**
TOTAL DAYS A CHILD/ CHILDREN LIVES IN MY HOME	**11,688-19,943**	**8255**	**28.27%**
TOTAL DAYS MARRIED AFTER CHILDREN LEAVE	**19,943-29,200**	**9277**	**31.75%**

The clock is ticking—my oldest daughter is thirteen and my son is eight.

Our time is limited. We only have so many hours, and even if we look at the days above, those are not real days. They do not account for sleeping, eating, school, and work. Right now, Monday through Friday, I see my children long enough to say goodbye to them before I go to work, and then (assuming that everyone is home and nothing is scheduled that night) I have the potential to see them for another three hours in the evening—but that is the maximum. We just do not have that much time together, and I bet your life looks similar.

How are we spending the time we have?

1. Are we growing in our relationship with the Lord and spending time with Him?
2. Are we intentionally spending time with our wives and our children—not just quality time, but quantity time too?
3. Does our job keep us from being at home? We are called to work and to support our families, so I am not saying do not work. Moreover, yes, sometimes our work may require us to travel, so I am not saying do not travel for work. However, if we hop on a plane on Sunday night and return on a plane Friday night week after week, we may need to evaluate if this is healthy or whether we need to look for a different job.
4. If we bring our work home or just come home late each evening, month after month and year after year, is it keeping us from spending time with our wives and our children?
5. Let's begin with the end in mind. If the Lord allows us to reach eighty years of age and we continue to live as we do today, what would be our biggest regret regarding the way we use our time?

The misery of it is, good things can become idols as well. Early in my marriage, before we had children, my wife and I were volunteering with a college ministry at our church. Circumstances changed and I had the opportunity to teach more at weekly campus meetings and on Sunday mornings with a Sunday school class, along with other time spent just ministering to the students throughout the week. It was good to be able to help them learn about Christ and to walk with them through a challenging season of life.

In my arrogance, I failed to notice the time I spent preparing for teaching and actually doing ministry was not spent with my wife. I was so focused on what I could do for the Lord (as if He needs anything from me), I overlooked the main relationship which I was called to foster and build: the relationship with my wife.

As I look back on that now, I realize I failed miserably. Even today I wrestle with time as I try to balance faith, family, and work. I try to make the correct choice, but I am not always joyful about it and I do not always make the right decisions. I need God's grace and the working of the Holy Spirit to help me rest in Him. He offers the same grace, discernment, and rest to you too.

These are hard questions that run counter to our culture, which says the more you work and the busier you stay, the better you are. It is easy to fall prey to this as a husband and father, saying, "Look at what I am doing for your benefit." Ask around and listen to how many children and wives want less stuff and more time together with their father or husband. You will find it is a substantial number.

HOW WE USE OUR MONEY

I know what you are thinking as you just read the subheading. It was bad enough that I mentioned time, but I had the audacity to mention money too. How you think about and use your money is a second key indicator of your allegiance and worship.

Money and income by themselves are neutral, meaning they are neither good nor bad. We can do good things with our money and be wise stewards of what the Lord has entrusted to us, or we can be reckless and foolish (time works the same way). Paul writes in his letter to Timothy,

But godliness with contentment is great gain, for we brought nothing into the world, and we cannot take anything out of the world. But if we have food and clothing, with these we will be content. But those who desire to be rich fall into temptation, into a snare, into many senseless and harmful desires that plunge people into ruin and destruction. For the love of money is a root of all kinds of evils. It is through this craving that some have wandered away from the faith and pierced themselves with many pangs (1 Timothy 6:6-10).

These phrases jump out to me:

- "we brought nothing into the world, and we cannot take anything out of the world"
- "those who desire to be rich fall into temptation, into a snare"
- "the love of money is the root of all kinds of evil."

All of these point out an internal motivation, a heart's desire that can lead us to worship something other than Christ. Money is not evil, having wealth is not sinful, but pursuing such things with a lustful longing will cause us to make bad decisions.

I wish I could say I was immune to this too, but that would be a lie. I wrestle with this each day and have gone through ruin and destruction because of my foolishness. My wife and I had been married about five years when this surfaced like a many-headed hydra in my life. My wife went through an extended illness and had to quit working. I did not know what to feel—I was sad, hurting, lonely, trying to encourage and support her and yet spinning for a loop too. The income dip had an impact on us, so I became afraid. We were making ends meet, but circumstances felt insurmountable. I tried to find a way to make more money while not increasing my hours at work, and got involved in real estate. Real estate can be a great investment when handled properly, but I was in too much of a hurry to do it wisely and to learn before jumping in with both feet. What followed were a couple of years of stress that nearly ended our marriage and ultimately led to bankruptcy.

My sin, arrogance, pride, selfishness—essentially my worship of the idol of money—brought not only me to ruin, but my wife as well.

How does money impact you and your family?

1. How does your use of money benefit or harm your family?
2. In what ways are you stewarding the money the Lord has given you?
3. In what ways are you worshipping or idolizing the money the Lord has given you?

I forgot what Matthew wrote:

> Therefore I tell you, do not be anxious about your life, what you will eat or what you will drink, nor about your body, what you will put on. Is not life more than food, and the body more than clothing? Look at the birds of the air: they neither sow nor reap nor gather into barns, and yet your heavenly Father feeds them. Are you not of more value than they? And which of you by being anxious can add a single hour to his span of life? And why are you anxious about clothing? Consider the lilies of the field, how they grow: they neither toil nor spin, yet I tell you, even Solomon in all his glory was not arrayed like one of these. But if God so clothes the

grass of the field, which today is alive and tomorrow is thrown into the oven, will he not much more clothe you, O you of little faith? Therefore do not be anxious, saying, "What shall we eat?" or "What shall we drink?" or "What shall we wear?" For the Gentiles seek after all these things, and your heavenly Father knows that you need them all. But seek first the kingdom of God and his righteousness, and all these things will be added to you. Therefore do not be anxious about tomorrow, for tomorrow will be anxious for itself. Sufficient for the day is its own trouble (Matthew 6:25-34).

As I look backwards, I think it was not forgetfulness on my part as much as I struggled to believe God's Word to be true. I mentally believed it, but that truth did not sink down into my heart—it was not actionable belief.

It reminds me of when I used to teach swim lessons. Some swimmers could swim, yet would not swim when they could not touch the bottom. This is what I was like—the person who understood God's Word but did not absorb it fully. Other swimmers could swim across the pool without any problems, regardless of the depth. They are like the person who knows and believes God's Word, which is evidenced in their life.

I trusted Christ for my salvation, but not for my provision. I thought the God of the Universe was going to leave me high-and-dry. I cannot even tell you how hard it is for me to write those words. I believed a lie about God and His character. This lie still lurks on the edges of my mind and Satan will throw it at me even to this day. I continually need to rest in the Lord and His provision and be reminded that He is a good Father who provides exactly what I need. What lies has money told you about God? Call it out for what it is—a lie—and replace that lie with Truth.

In the last couple of months, I have read two books on George Mueller which have really challenged me. Mueller was a pastor in England during the 1800's. He started a ministry that took care of orphans who otherwise would have been relegated to workhouses. His ministry funded schools not only in England, but also in other countries around the world, during a time in history when public schools did not exist as they do today. His ministry also funded Sunday Schools and other missions work.

The amazing thing is not what the Lord accomplished through Mueller, though that is praiseworthy, but how and why Mueller did what he did. He began a children's home to care for children who had no place to go *in order to show the world that God was real and that He answered prayer.* Mueller wanted to make much of the Lord and trusted that the Lord would provide.

Mueller did not ask anyone for any money to fund this ministry, and the people who worked in the ministry did not ask anyone either. Instead, he prayed (and they prayed) and asked that the Lord would make Himself known.

Sometimes they had just enough to cover expenses and received it on the day it was needed. There were seasons without surplus, but the children in his care never lacked food or clothing, they never went without a meal or a place to sleep or people to care for them. Thousands of children had changed lives because the Lord responded to a man who saw God for who He is.

Too often I get caught up in the "stuff" of the world or in trying to make sure my family has enough savings for retirement and college and—just fill in the blank. The Lord is gracious and faithful, even when our faith wavers, and for that I am overwhelmingly thankful. We need to be diligent with our finances and not careless because all things belong to the Lord and we just take care of them for a while. We need to be good stewards, but we need to make sure we worship the Lord who provides the money—not the money itself. A steward manages resources for an owner, but does not own the resources.

- Do you consider yourself a steward of your money or the owner of your money?
- Where is God inviting you to be a good steward?
- How can you worship the One who provides instead of the provision?

HOW WE FOCUS OUR ATTENTION

A third area that comes to mind when I think about sowing and reaping is what activities draw our attention or focus. It could be lumped under the category of time, but I think it is important to separate it into its own section. Why? Because it can include our time, but it also includes our thoughts. Things that draw our attention can range from a football game on a Sunday afternoon to taking our children to their activities, from hobbies to side-jobs, and even movies.

Football games and hobbies are not sinful in and of themselves, and can actually be quite enjoyable. Taking our children to activities or coaching their teams can give us the chance to pour not only into the lives of our children, but also into the lives of others around us. Side-jobs can be helpful to provide needed income for our families. Trying to launch a business in our spare time while keeping our day job can be beneficial because it allows us to maintain a stable stream of income.

The bigger issue is what impact these things have on our families and our walk with the Lord if they take too much of our attention or take the place of God. Do our wives become "football widows" during football season when we spend our weekends and weeknights so focused on a game that we ignore the precious bride entrusted to us by the Lord? Do our children's activities keep us so busy that we do not have time to be a family or attend church on the weekends? Do we find ourselves trying to live through our children as they perform? Does a side-job keep us away from home or, even if we are physically at home, does it direct our attention and focus elsewhere?

I was reminded of this lately as I have been trying to complete some projects around my home. Maybe you feel the same way about never-ending house projects. It is a tough balance of trying to take care of our homes and spend time with our families. Looking back over the last few years, summer seems to be the season when I try to accomplish tasks around the house, like painting or small remodeling projects. I am in the midst of trying to complete a couple of small ones right now so that I can start on some bookshelves and cabinets in the near future, hopefully finishing them before school starts.

I am not a professional, but simply learning as I go, which means some things take extra time. I am not consumed with these things year-round, but I try to focus on them for just a short period. In the midst of this, my son has come up to me several times during the last week and asked me to go play in the backyard on our trampoline. Each time he does this, I need to pause and ask myself a question: **What is most important in this moment?** There are some evenings when I am trying to get the grass mowed ahead of the rain and must finish before I can play. There are other times when I need to take or pick up one of my daughters from practice and will need to play later. However, I also must stop and ask if it is more important to take an extra day (or two...or three...or a week) to complete a house project in order to spend time with my children when they ask me, or is it more important to get the work done right now.

As men, you and I need to keep our attention focused on Christ, and then allow the Holy Spirit to lead our actions accordingly. One of the hardest things for me is to take the necessary corrective measures when I see that I am leading poorly (or not leading at all). I enjoy watching football in the fall, but there are weekends when I do not catch a game. I want my children to be involved in activities, but even more than that, I want them learning about Christ and being able to be a child for a little while longer. They will grow up, and I want them to grow up and move out because the Lord has designed us this way. I want to do what I can to make sure they are ready when that time comes, but I also know they need to be children for a season when they are young and not force-fitted into adulthood when they are eight. The next time your kids ask you to play, ask yourself "What is most important at this moment?" Or, let's go one step further and ask "What will matter most in five years?"

Our attention can also be drawn to things that are not good, but quite the opposite—things that are sinful and destructive. Escapism in a broad definition would be something which allows us to temporarily escape from reality and shift to something we think is better. It can take all kinds of shapes and hues, ranging from innocent things like books and movies, to harmful things like pornography and substance abuse. Yes, those are very broad topics and I cannot begin to cover all of their facets, however, let's at least bring them up for discussion to shed some light on them.

If you read the novel *Ready Player One*,[2] you read about a game called the Oasis, which became the center of business and life for the characters in the book. For someone to go into the Oasis meant a complete escape from the real world around them. It consumed everyone. We have online worlds in our culture that can do the same thing, pulling us down the rabbit hole and allowing us to get involved in many things outside the people around us. We can lose ourselves completely.

I am a huge fan of books and movies. I always have two or three books floating around in my car and piles at home. Books and movies are not sinful in and of themselves (depending on the content). However, if they are used as a means to consistently step out of the real world, they become like a drug. There were periods of my life where I struggled because life was hard, and I would retreat into fiction or movies as a reprieve from the tough circumstances around me. It was easier to read a book than to work through job problems or find a different job. It was more enjoyable to catch part of a movie than to spend time with my wife when she was going through health problems.

In the same way, I struggled with alcohol. Alcohol by itself is not sinful if consumed in moderation and done so according to the law. As we all know, consuming too much alcohol at any one time can lead to problems because it removes the mental boundaries and guard rails the Lord has given us for our safety. This is one reason why drunkenness is sinful (Ephesians 5:18). I did not go to bars to drink or out with friends. I started drinking to alleviate stress and anxiety, and it helped a little for a while. However, instead of learning to press through the difficulties and work towards solutions, I escaped with another drink.

I struggled with alcohol before I was married, but when I met my wife, I realized I needed to change. The Lord helped me walk away from it and stay sober for several years. A few years later, we went through a hard time in our marriage because of work and my wife's health concerns, like I mentioned before. I thought following Christ meant there would be no setbacks and hardships, or at least they would be different hardships than what we were experiencing. My theology was deeply flawed, and maybe part of your heart believes that tempting lie too.

Instead of turning to the Lord and resting in Him, I slipped back into drinking just to take the edge off the anxiety. I blamed others instead of owning my junk, and so I escaped with alcohol coupled with books and movies.

Of course, a little led to a lot and I nearly destroyed our marriage. My actions definitely scarred it for many years. If you fall into a pattern of escapism, your marriage and family are likely on the line as well. God delivered me from that pit, but He did not do it overnight. By His grace, I quit drinking again and then began to work through my own issues with help. Asking for help on anything is hard for me, whether I am asking how to solve a problem at work or how to fix something around the house. It is hard because in my head, I think I should know everything or be able to fix everything on my own. Such a belief in myself is wanton pride and arrogance because I am a *dependent* being—dependent on God for life, breath, strength, and everything else. Maybe you struggle with feelings like this, too. I have learned it is far better to ask for help than to wander around in pain or ignorance.

Consider your forms of escapism, and then take a deeper look at what it's covering up. For me, drinking was not at the heart of the issue. It was simply something to mask my desire to escape. The heart issue was that I did not trust the Lord.

How often do you seek "me" time and how do you use it?

1. When you retreat, what is the motivation for doing so? To rest? To reflect? To not have to think about life?
2. How can too much escapism lead to relationship struggles with your family?
3. In what ways do we use escapism to try to avoid responsibility?

For guys, pornography is a common escape mechanism. Pornography robs us of the beauty and design of marriage while heavily laying guilt and shame upon us. It distorts what God calls good and twists our thinking and feeling, corrupting our ideas and thoughts and wreaking havoc upon our families. It also makes a wife feel like she does not measure or is not wanted. The challenge is that pornography taps into those desires, feelings, and hormones which the Lord has given us for our wives, and turns them into something else.

In fact, a physiological high occurs when we view pornography for the first time or return to it after much time away. Studies have found that pornography usage has effects similar to drug addiction, including tolerance build-up and escalation.[3] In reality, pornography is no different from any deadly crutch of escapism. They all deliver guilt, shame, distorted thinking, sneaky feelings, and they all exchange the Truth for a lie.

In some churches, it can be taboo to discuss the difficulties of avoiding or wrestling with pornography. And in some churches, it can be taboo to discuss any form of escapism. If you are struggling with pornography, find someone you can trust (an elder, a mature follower of Christ) and talk with them. Get some accountability for the behavior, and bolster the courage to deal with the root issues, because the pornography is just a symptom of something deeper.

Our attention can be pulled in so many directions, sometimes good and sometimes bad, sometimes healthy and sometimes harmful. We need to be aware of where our attention resides. Pray frequently to the Lord and be vigilant with your attention because Satan will gladly lure you away without your awareness.

Have you ever heard of a plumb bob? It has been used for centuries in construction, even dating back to the Ancient Egyptians. It is a simple level or measuring device consisting of a piece of metal or a weighted object with a point that you tie on the end of a piece of string. If you want to see if a point is directly above or below something, you hold one end of the string to a mark and let the plumb bob dangle at the other. When it quits moving, you know you are perfectly perpendicular or vertically level—the measurement is considered plumb or true.

When we evaluate the fruit produced from our time, money, and attention, it is like using a plumb bob on our spiritual walk. If any of these three things are not centered on the Lord, we will be out of plumb, and our relationship with the Lord and our families will suffer. Remember, time, money, and attention are neutral, meaning they are neither good nor bad. The fruit from their use will tell us the seeds we are sowing.

QUICK HITS FROM THE CHAPTER

● Time is a great equalizer for all of us because we have the same amount of time each day. We need to be good stewards of our time and use it for what God says is best.

● Money is neither good nor bad, however, it can lead us to do foolish things, to value it above God. We need to remember that we are only the stewards of this resource and not the owner.

● Our attention can be pulled to many things, both good and bad. We need to be aware of our thoughts and focus to ensure that we are pursuing the best things according to God's plan.

● We need to take inventory of our lives and evaluate (honestly) who we are worshipping. This can be on a daily or minute-by-minute basis.

QUESTIONS FOR REFLECTION

1. What kind of fruit do you think you are producing? How do the results of your current actions (the fruit) compare with what you think you are producing?

2. What did you learn about time, money, and attention from your father? From other men around you?

3. As you look at your life today, what kind of seeds are you sowing based on your words and actions, and what kind of fruit are you expecting to grow from those seeds?

CHAPTER 3

Pause and Realign

How are you doing at this point? The fact that you are still reading tells me you want to know more. You may have no issues with what we have just covered, you may wrestle with all of it, or you may struggle with parts of it. I would hazard a guess that you have struggled with most or all of it at some point in time—maybe not every day, but some days. You're not alone—I have struggled and continue to struggle too, which is why I am right here with you. We can do this together. Remember, some days we will have great success and some days we will fall flat on our faces (I assume it will happen to you because it happens to me).

Be gracious with yourself, cry out to the Lord, and remember the Holy Spirit is at work in you. Above all, we have to remind each other to keep moving forward. We want to be farther along next year than we are today and we want to be farther along five years from now than we are next year.

PAUSE FOR ENCOURAGEMENT

You can probably tell by now I'm a big fan of books and movies, and that includes Tolkien's *The Lord of the Rings*. Théoden was one of the fascinating characters in the series who could be a great encouragement to us. He was the king of the land of Rohan, a people known for their horses and their riders. We first encounter this frail old man who can barely hold himself up in a chair part way through the second book in the series, *The Two Towers*.[4] He was a king, who, over time, fell prey to bad counsel. The evil designs of a rebellious wizard took its toll on him. When Gandalf, Aragorn, Legolas, and Gimli (aka the good guys) show up to bring help and warning, things change. The evil powers were driven out and Théoden stood tall once more. Not only did he stand, but he was now able to wield his sword and lead his people into battle.

In the third book, *The Return of the King*, Théoden's knights followed him into battle on the Pelennor Fields where he was ultimately killed (sorry for the spoiler).[5] His actions changed the course of the battle, but more than the battle, his actions changed the course of his people.

Pause and consider which Théoden best describes you right now: are you a frail old man who can barely hold himself up in a chair, or are you able to stand strong, carry your sword, and lead your people well? Maybe you find yourself in both positions, like a weak man at home yet a strong one in the office.

Before we continue, it's important that you genuinely recognize where you are right now. Genuine growth stems from a realistic perception of the here-and-now.

You see, no matter where you are now, you have the opportunity to step forward. Do not think you need to be perfect in order to begin—you can start today. If you feel as feeble as Théoden, you can regain your strength through the Lord. If you're walking as proudly as a king in victory, you can continue in triumph. Starting today, this minute, you can honor and serve the Lord and love and serve your family. Wield your sword, bravely lead your family, and make sure your life is aligned to humbly serve your King.

Let's do this together.

REALIGN YOUR TIME, MONEY, AND ATTENTION

If you are like me, my head and heart tell me many different things. I can rationalize my time, money, and attention in all kinds of ways, and yet, if changes need to occur, I am being disobedient to ignore the Lord.

But enough talk for the moment! *We must act.* Remember, realigning does not simply mean identifying problems, but making purposeful effort to correct the issue once it is known. When I take my car to the mechanic and ask them to realign my wheels, they do not raise it up on the lift, see that the wheels are out of whack, say "Yep, things are crooked," and give it back to me. If they did, I would be upset because nothing changed—the wheels are still crooked. Instead, when they see the wheels need correcting, they physically make the adjustment so the wheels roll straight. The same process works for us today. Again, *we must act!* I say this as much to me as to you because I frequently acknowledge my need to do something, but then struggle to implement change.

Now that we have talked through three tough areas of our lives (time, money, and attention), let's do something that takes courage.

- Step 1: Pray and ask the Lord to show us where we need to change.
- Step 2: Be willing to change what the Lord shows us and identify the first step necessary to make those changes.
- Step 3: Begin the change.

Determine which step you are on right now and talk with another guy who can keep you accountable. Remember, accountability is not a bad word, nor is it punishment. Accountability simply allows us to encourage one another on the journey because we cannot do it alone. Speaking of encouragement, let me encourage you with a few specific examples of steps one through three.

IF TIME IS A PROBLEM

Step 1: Pray to the Lord, asking, "Lord, will You please show me where I need to change?"

- If work keeps us away from home too much of each month, do we need to look for a different job that will allow us to be at home more, even if it means a step back in our careers?
- Do we need to ask our employers for alternate options like telecommuting?
- Do we need to learn how to delegate some tasks that are of lesser importance?

Step 2: Are you willing to make changes? What is the first step?

Step 3: Enact change. Follow through and ask someone to keep you accountable.

IF MONEY IS A PROBLEM

Step 1: Pray to the Lord, asking, "Lord, will You please show me where I need to change?"

- How am I looking for money to fix my problems and make my life better?
- What possessions or quests for possessions are keeping me from being generous to God's work?
- How am I looking at my money and possessions to measure my status compared to those around me?
- How do I view them as tools given to me by the Lord to use for His work?

Step 2: Are you willing to make changes? What is the first step?

Step 3: Enact change. Follow through and ask someone to keep you accountable.

IF ATTENTION IS A PROBLEM

Step 1: Pray to the Lord, asking, "Lord, will You please show me where I need to change?"

- On what do I think and focus my attention most frequently?
- How does my attention center upon the Lord and His purposes?
- What activities pull me away from the Lord and from my family, and what can I do to change my behavior?

Step 2: Are you willing to make changes? What is the first step?

Step 3: Enact change. Follow through and ask someone to keep you accountable.

Yes, this is incredibly radical and unpopular, and I can picture you turning on your heels and running in the opposite direction.

Here's the thing: If we become vice president of a Fortune 500 company or build a business from scratch to an IPO and our marriages fall apart, we have failed. If our work consumes us and we do not spend time and effort with our children, we have failed. Even if it is good work like serving the needy, taking the Gospel to the hard places of the world, caring for the sick and destitute—should we ignore our homes in the process, we have failed.

If we are consumed with possessions and money, we need to take a step back and let it go, seeking the Lord and the wisdom that comes from His Word. We need to remember that we are simply stewards of what has been given to us, not its master.

If our hobbies and other interests consume our time or pull us away from our families, we need to reevaluate their importance.

We have covered a lot of ground in a short time, and we need to pause at this fork in the road. Success and failure are the two options. Does your journey need a realignment? It's easier to plot a course from right here than to reroute later down the road. If you are ready, let's look at some action steps down the path of success that can help us lead well at home.

QUICK HITS FROM THE CHAPTER

- Frequent evaluation is critical to maintaining our walk with the Lord. We need to adjust our lives accordingly to ensure that we are following what the Lord wants us to do.

- Where you are today is not where you have to be next year or five years from now. There is hope, so be strong and courageous, but we must *act*. Théoden acted, and so must we if we want change to occur.

QUESTIONS FOR REFLECTION

1. Where do you struggle most: time, money, or attention?

2. Where would your wife say you struggle most: time, money, attention?

3. What is one action that your wife would say would be most helpful to realign your life to follow Christ better?

4. From the end of the chapter, how did you answer the three steps to any one of the areas (time, money, attention)?

   a. Step 1: Pray to the Lord, asking "Lord, please show me where I need to change?"

   b. Step 2: Are you willing to make changes? What is the first step?

   c. Step 3: Enact change. Follow through and ask someone to keep you accountable.

CHAPTER 4

Laying the Groundwork

The next time you enter a building, pause for a moment and notice the foundation of the structure. As I sit at my kitchen table, I do not notice anything out of the ordinary—everything feels stable. The walls are upright, the roof does not shake, and the structure is sound. Do you want to know why? The foundation is level and well laid. Structures with poor foundations will collapse over time (some quicker than others), but solid foundations allow for straight walls and sturdy roofs (although I'll allow the Leaning Tower of Pisa to be a rare exception).

We just paused and realigned our priorities, and now let's look inward and evaluate our own foundation before we go forward. Our foundation does not have to be complete like the foundation of a building. However, we do need to begin with ourselves before discussing how to serve our wife and children.

As you read this chapter, appraise yourself and see if you already have these habits. If so, praise the Lord! You have a good start. If not, praise the Lord! You are now aware and can initiate growth.

BE PRESENT WITH YOUR TIME AT HOME

We talked about the challenge of using our time wisely, so let's circle back to that point. How do we improve our time spent at home? In a moment, I will walk you through a typical week in my home as an example, but first let's go through some questions that will help you evaluate your own week. There is no judgment or condemnation here—we are simply making a list and answering honestly. I'm assuming you have a traditional Monday through Friday daytime work schedule, but please adjust these questions to fit your personal work schedule.

- What does a typical work day look like for you? When do you get up, go to work, come home?
- What does a typical evening look like for you? How do you usually spend your time? Who and what gets your attention?
- How much time each day/week do you spend focusing on the Lord (reading your Bible, praying, teaching your family)?
- Do you biblically mentor other men? Are you being mentored by someone?

Okay, this is a typical week in my home, but I must confess that the older my children get, the less "typical" each week becomes.

I wake up around 6:00 a.m. and get ready to go to work (shower, shave, brush my teeth, etc.). I then go downstairs to make breakfast and get my lunch together. I will likely see one of my daughters up before I leave. But apart from that, I tell my wife goodbye and go to work. I drive to work, start working about 8:00 a.m., take an hour for lunch, and then drive home around 5:00 p.m.

When I get home, I drop my laptop and coat, change clothes (yes, just like Mr. Rogers—though no cardigan), and try to begin engaging my family. This requires me to be present physically (I am in the house) but also mentally, and it is the mental part that is the hardest. Do you sometimes feel the same way after a full day at work?

I love my wife and children and enjoy being with them, but depending on the day, I just want to disengage and be alone. You know what it's like to have your mind stuck on work and not on what's happening at home. However, that is not good for me or my family. When we sit down for dinner (if no one is going to a rehearsal or practice), I try to look up from my food and ask questions to each of my children. "What was your favorite subject today? What neat thing did you learn today? How did your (fill in the blank activity) go?" If I'm honest, I don't always do this. Sometimes I still just look at my plate. However, if I am to lead well, my frustrations with work and life should not be directed toward my wife and children because it is not their fault. I am a guarded person, so sharing feelings does not come naturally to me, but I am learning how to show my humanity to my children by revealing how events or conversations affect me emotionally.

For example, we were recently evaluating whether to buy a different house. We found one we really liked and took the kids to look at it. My wife and I then went back to look at it again to re-evaluate it. Afterwards, my wife and I looked closely at the financial impact of the move, such as exactly how much our mortgage payment, utilities, and other expenses would change. We prayed about it, asking the Lord to give us wisdom, and thought about it for a couple of days. Finally, we decided *not* to make an offer. I was really disappointed and frustrated, but it was the correct decision and looking back on it now, I do not regret it. Once we made the decision, we sat down with our children and told them how we came to our conclusion. I shared my own personal feelings of disappointment in the result and how I was struggling with those feelings. I wanted them to see (and to remind myself) it is okay to feel disappointed and sad, but even in disappointment, the Lord is still in control.

Okay, back to the dinner table. After dinner, we clean up and then I try to spend time with one or more children doing something intentional. (We will discuss more specific examples of intentional activities in the following chapters.) Sometimes I fill the time with chores or other projects around the house, although it is more important for me to spend time with my wife and children than to work on things. If tonight is the only time I can spend reading with my daughter this week because she has rehearsals the next two nights, then I prioritize reading with her instead of mowing the grass.

Later in the evening, before bed, I lead a devotional time with my children. We take anywhere from fifteen to thirty minutes to read, talk, and pray. When my children were younger, we would read different children's Bibles (See the Vault of Books, Food, and Fun at the end of the book for specific titles). We have read each of them many times and I would highly recommend them as a place to start with your children. Lately, we have been reading a chapter of the gospels each night and talking through it. Last year we also started going through Operation World, where we pray for a different country each night. Please hear me though—I aim for this every night of the week, but I'm a work in progress just like you. We miss some nights when family visits or we go out of town or when events run late.

Life is amazingly complex, and even more so when we relate to other people. Think of life like this: if you are only responsible for you, meaning you as an adult man are responsible for only you (single, no children), you have a life complexity equal to 10. If you get married, your life becomes more complicated—good but complicated. However, the complexity does not double. It increases exponentially.

What I mean is that if you start out at 10, adding your wife does not mean it is 10 x 2 = 20, it becomes 10^2 or 10 x 10 = 100. The moment you add a child, complexity now goes to 10^3 or 10 x 10 x 10 = 1000. A second child leads you to 10^4 or 10 x 10 x 10 x 10 = 10,000, and so on. This is why when you have one less child on a weekend because they are at a retreat, life seems so much easier—the house is not empty, but you have a moment with exponentially less complexity in your life.

LIFE COMPLEXITY	
YOU	10^1 OR 10 X 1 = 10
YOU AND YOUR WIFE	10^2 OR 10 X 10 = 100
YOU, YOUR WIFE, ONE CHILD	10^3 OR 10 X 10 X 10 = 1000
YOU, YOUR WIFE, TWO CHILDREN	10^4 OR 10 X 10 X 10 X 10 = 10,000
YOU, YOUR WIFE, THREE CHILDREN	10^5 OR 10 X 10 X 10 X 10 X 10 = 100,000

You've heard me repeatedly say that I am a huge fan of marriage and children, so please do not misunderstand me. I just want us to see that life is complicated, so we need to be intentional in how we approach our families. Otherwise we will feel very overwhelmed and want to check out. The Lord equips us for this, even when we do not "feel" like it (remember, feelings can be fickle). If we are followers of Christ, the Holy Spirit dwells within us and is our guarantee of our inheritance from the Lord. The Holy Spirit will also help us to engage with our families when we ask Him. The Lord will change our hearts and attitudes and motivate us to invest richly at home.

Take one action of intentionality today in regards to your time at home. Can you ask each member of your family one question at dinner? Can you read a bible story with your family before bed? Can you observe your family and try to identify one interest that each person has?

YOU CANNOT TEACH WHAT YOU DO NOT KNOW

I taught English at a small classical Christian school, and was then asked to also teach first year Latin. I did not know Latin when I agreed to do this. In order to teach it, I had to learn the subject. No, I was not a Latin scholar—I could not pick up a historical text written in Latin and translate it without dictionaries or other sources. However, I was able to learn it well enough to understand and teach it. Although I did not master the entire language before stepping into the classroom, I learned the material on my own and then gained greater insight as I taught it and pushed ahead with my learning.

Through this process I learned a valuable truth—I could not teach what I did not know. I needed to learn the material well enough to apply it and explain it to someone else so they could understand it. Yet I didn't need to be a master before I began teaching. In fact, we will gain more mastery as we teach because there is only so much we can learn ahead of time. Many times we will learn far more on the job than we can learn in preparation for the job.

A friend of mine shared a story with me about his job training. He worked as a customer and technical support specialist. His job was to answer calls from customers who either had questions about their services and equipment or who needed help trouble-shooting a problem. When he was hired, he had twelve focused weeks of training. He was in a cohort of new hires, and each of them learned as much as they could in the classroom and by shadowing other specialists as they served customers on the phone. At the end of the twelve weeks, when they were about to move out of training and step into a full-time role, the trainer congratulated them on their work and then told them they probably knew about ten percent of everything they needed for the job. The rest of their knowledge could only come by doing the job, answering the questions on the spot, and finding the answers.

Just like my friend needed *some* information to start his job, he could not know *everything* before he started. In the same way, we do not have to master the Bible before we start going through it with our family. *The most important part is to start.*

Leading devotional times with our children requires us to learn as we go along. We may feel uncomfortable reading the Bible with our kids because we do not know it well or we do not know how it all fits together. I understand. I know it can be daunting when my children ask me a question and I am not sure of the right answer or how to explain the answer. As a dad, I sometimes mistakenly think I have to know all the answers, but the reality is I do not know everything- I don't even come close. My kid's questions force me to learn and ask questions of my own so I can go back to them with information.

Do you know enough to take the first step? What do you have to learn on your own before you can begin leading your family? *Remember, the most important part is to start.* Keep a notepad or a notes app with you as you go through the Bible with your family. Write down all of the questions that come up. Have your family write down their questions too. See if you can find answers within the Bible, or ask one of the elders or pastors at your church for suggestions on finding the answers.

READING YOUR BIBLE

One place to start learning is by sitting down each day and reading the Bible. If you have never read it cover-to-cover, this can be very intimidating, but my encouragement to you is this: just start. Be gracious with yourself and try to read one chapter each day, or plan to read at least five days a week.

If you do not want to read the Bible from beginning to end in order, a simple web search will offer many reading plans that will walk you through the Bible in a variety of ways. One I have found very useful is *The Discipleship Journal Bible Reading Plan*[6] created by Navigators. It walks you through short portions of Scripture from different parts of the Bible each day. It also provides grace days during the month, meaning when you look at January, it has twenty-five reading days, even though there are thirty-one days in the month. I try to read four chapters a day, five days a week from this plan. If you have never read the Bible before, this plan might be the most helpful one because it gives you specific readings and a variety of texts. The readings are more than one chapter a day, but they do provide valuable structure.

A word of encouragement—if you fall behind, *do not give up!* Pick it up tomorrow. If you are following a plan, skip ahead to the current day (yes, you have permission to do this). The goal is *growth not perfection.* We are sinners, which is why we need a Savior. We do not gain brownie points or merit badges by trying to be perfect.

Members of my small group have recommended a few audio Bible apps that will read the Bible to you. I have not personally used these, but they would be great for your morning commute to work or even to listen to while you follow along in the text. As

for flexibility because life happens and schedules
anged. It is okay to be flexible with it and to adju
doing, whether it is switching studies or modifyi
ou meet. It can also be good if you set start and en
e meetings, meaning you can plan to meet twice a
six months and then see where to go from there. It
ave to be a weekly event for life.

a mentor who can help you grow in your walk. This
someone who is helping you learn more about how to
others, how to grow in your role as a husband, or simply
help you take the next few steps in your sanctification
And as you grow, seek out a younger man whom you
entor.

an English speaker, I struggle to pronounce some of the names
and places in the Bible. Sometimes it sounds like I am trying to
talk with a mouthful of marbles as I attempt to read names like
Mahershalalhashbaz (son of Isaiah) and Zaphnathpaneah (the
Egyptian name given to Joseph). Hearing a proper pronunciation
can help our understanding and comprehension—plus it's just
fun to hear those complicated names!

The goal is to learn the whole broad story of scripture and to see
the Lord for who He is and what He has done. As you journey
through the Bible, follow these tips:

- Pray each time you sit down to read. Ask the Holy Spirit
  to open your eyes and mind to what He would have you
  learn and apply that day.

- Keep a notebook nearby for any questions that come up
  while you read. You can jot them down and either try to
  look them up yourself or if you are not sure where to start,
  find a trusted person at your church who can help you.

- As you read, keep in mind the basic framework of God's
  story: creation, fall, redemption, restoration.

- Remember the Old Testament points ahead to Jesus while
  the New Testament tells the events of His life on earth
  (Matthew, Mark, Luke, and John), the history of the
  early church, instructions to the church, and the return
  of Christ.

A quick note on Bibles: buying one can be overwhelming
with all of the different translations and types. To help in this
process, I recommend that you acquire a study Bible. They
contain commentaries and notes on the various passages, along
with maps and summaries. The notes and summaries are not
God's Word, so it is important not to confuse the two. However,

they can be very helpful as you read. I currently use The ESV Study Bible, but I have also used the NIV Study Bible and the Apologetics Study Bible (HCSB translation).

MENTORING OTHER MEN

As we grow in our walk with the Lord, we also need to learn from other men who have walked this path longer than we have. Jesus' last command to His disciples before He ascended into heaven at the end of Matthew is to "Go therefore and make disciples of all nations, baptizing them in the name of the Father and of the Son and of the Holy Spirit, teaching them to observe all that I have commanded you. And behold, I am with you always, to the end of the age" (Matthew 28:19-20).

A disciple is defined as a learner, so when Jesus says to "make disciples," He is telling us to make learners. And what should these learners learn? That's right! All that Jesus commanded us. How will they learn it though? They will learn by watching us and listening to us. So how do we learn? You guessed it! We learn by watching and listening to other men who are farther along in their walk with Christ.

Let's model our relationships after the examples of Paul, Barnabas, and Timothy in the New Testament. Paul mentored Timothy so that he could in turn lead churches and mentor other men. Timothy learned from Paul and then applied what he learned. Paul and Barnabas served together and encouraged one another.

Do you have a mentor like Paul? How about a close peer for mutual encouragement like Barnabas? What about someone to mentor like Timothy?

I have gone long stretches w
those seasons were hard. Dur,
to learn from a godly man in o
encouragement to me by meetin,
have coffee and he asks how I an
and mentally. He asks about my fa
am doing with them. I ask him ques
in my life and walk. I share where I a
am trying to do. He prays for and with
me get farther along in my sanctificatio.
sanctification is the process of becoming
Holy Spirit works in us). He even checks
our coffee meetings to see how things are g
me grow in my walk with the Lord by provi
for my own growth and how to best lead my s
discuss the progress of the group and he helps
to encourage them in their walk with Christ. I ca
say that I would not be the leader that I am today
this mentor.

I have also had the opportunity to mentor a few guys
along the things I have learned. In one instance, I met
one guy every other week at lunch and we went throug
books together over the span of a year. In another instanc
met with a guy each week for coffee for about six months
he was going through a really hard time in his life. I listene
encouraged him with Scripture, and tried to be a sounding be
for him. Another time I met with two guys about once a mont
the evenings and we went through a study together.

One of the challenges for me in each case was remembering I
did not have to do it perfectly. Fear definitely makes me hesitate.
I need to be reminded to take heart and not be afraid because I
am afraid of making mistakes and doing something wrong. I also

had to allow
need to be cl
what you ar
how often y
dates for th
month for
does not l

Seek out
could be
mentor
how to
walk.
can m

QUICK HITS FROM THE CHAPTER

- If the foundation of a building is not solid, the building will crumble. Our walk with the Lord must be the starting point of our relationship with our family.

- We all have the same amount of time each day and each week. It is crucial for us to be aware of how we spend our time and how it can seep away without us realizing it.

- We can only teach what we know, which means we need to grow in our walk with Christ in order to effectively teach our families about Him and model a relationship with Him.

- One key activity that can greatly increase our knowledge of the Lord is reading our Bible. Use a Bible reading plan to help guide your journey or read through a few chapters of the Bible each day.

- Mentoring other men in Christ and being mentored by other godly men bolsters our sanctification walk as we learn how to deepen our relationship with Christ and how to strengthen the relationships with our family members.

QUESTIONS FOR REFLECTION

1. What changes do I need to make in my daily/ weekly schedule to ensure that I am growing in my sanctification walk?

2. How can I improve my daily time with the Lord?

3. What Bible reading plan do I need to start following today?

4. Who is one man that I respect and who is solid in their faith that I might ask to mentor me?

5. Am I far enough along in my faith walk to mentor someone else?

CHAPTER 5

Be Present with Your Wife

Your relationship to Christ is the most important relationship in your life. The second most important relationship is with your wife. Remember, the easy way to measure value and importance in your life is to ask, "Where do I spend my time, money, and attention?" Therefore, I need to routinely evaluate whether I am apportioning my time to reflect my wife's high rank. Does she receive the time and attention from me that she warrants?

BE INTENTIONAL WITH YOUR WIFE

Even though life is complicated, that does not give us a pass with our family. Find ways to be intentional in spending time with your wife based on her interests, likes, shared activities, etc. Obviously cost is a major factor in what you can do. I am not saying you have to spend a fortune on activities or "stuff," but you do need to try to find some connection with your wife that fits her, not you.

If you do not have children, it is much easier to spend intentional time with your wife. I did not say it was easy, but it can be *easier*. If you are considering having children, now is the time to make this a habit because when children do arrive, they have a way of consuming the balance of your time.

One way I have found to be intentional with my wife is to sit down at the end of the day, once all of our children are in bed, set aside my electronics, and ask about her day. Because of schedules, this does not happen every night, but I try to do this as often as possible. In the past, we have tried to sit down at different times during the day, but have found the best time is once all of the children are in bed. If you were going to sit down with your wife everyday, what time do you think would work best?

We homeschool our children, so I ask how school went with each of our children. I also ask about other things in her life, from relationships to church, from her emotions to her heart. My goal is to ask questions and listen. Listening is the key, but I must confess that I do not always do it correctly. Often, your wife just wants you to listen, not try to solve a problem.

Another way to be intentional with your wife is to regularly take her out on a date. The best way to do this is to put it on your calendar and then aim to make it happen—because it will not happen spontaneously. My wife and I do not do this frequently enough, but it is something we seek to do once every two to three months. As our children get older and can stay home by themselves, we hope to go on more dates together. I know some couples go on a date every month or even every week. There is no hard and fast rule, but the main thing is just to do it. It does not have to be expensive. Going out for coffee or ice cream is a wonderful thing. Go for a walk or hike, go window-shopping at a store your wife likes, watch a matinee or go to a bookstore or a museum. What you do is not nearly as important as being intentional and letting your wife know that she is important to you by spending time together. Consult your family schedule, then pick a day right now, add it to your calendar, and think of an enjoyable activity to do with your wife.

A third suggestion is to pray with your wife on a regular basis. Being able to pray aloud together for things that are on your hearts is extremely important. As a husband, we are called to lead well, and to lead in this case means we need to initiate prayer time. If this is not something you do on a regular basis, put it on the calendar for once or twice a week until it becomes a habit. Increase frequency as it becomes easier. Also, there is no pressure to pray for ten minutes. Why don't you try praying for thirty seconds with your wife today. If you don't know what to say, you can simply thank the Lord for loving you both and for your marriage, then ask Him to protect your marriage and help you to follow Him.

Lastly, go through a devotional or read through the Bible together. It does not have to be heavy or deeply intellectual, and it does not have to take a long time. The key purpose is to do something that points you toward the Lord. Try reading a Psalm together each day for a month, or pick one of the gospels (Luke and John are my favorites) and read a chapter a night. If you miss a night, be gracious with yourself, but try again the next day. Remember, we are aiming for growth and growth is usually incremental. We are also aiming to love and lead our wife well.

BE EMOTIONALLY PRESENT
WITH CHORES

As a husband, what do you do around the house? Too often men are portrayed as lazy and lethargic, sitting in front of a screen and vegging out when they get home from work. Unfortunately, that can be the picture of what happens in the home with some men. But let's be true leaders who play an active role in our homes.

I think a better question is: how do you serve your family when you are home? Do you look around in the evenings and on the weekends and think, "What can I do that would make life easier for my wife?" Is it cleaning? Cooking? Spending time with our children? Going to the grocery store? Mowing the grass?

You may think that you and your wife are in agreement on who handles (or should handle) specific tasks around your house. However, that may not be true, but only assumed. You may assume that she will always empty the dishwasher, but she might assume that you will occasionally empty it when you notice that it's clean. Even if she doesn't assume this, you will earn brownie points for doing it! You may assume that she will clean the bathrooms when she assumes that you will clean the bathrooms.

For some men, I believe that this idea is new and foreign to your way of thinking. In either case, I would encourage you this week to start observing what is accomplished around your home and by whom. Then, have a conversation with your wife about this and listen to her ideas, opinions, and suggestions. Ask what you can do to make sure you are serving her at home in a way that is helpful to her. Be willing to do something different—take a risk and learn something new. Ask her what she would like and then work together to make a plan. This is not a one-size-fits-all kind of deal—have the conversation together and listen well. (In case you haven't noticed, the art of listening is a large part of being a good husband and father.) The plan can change over time because your life situation three years or even three months from now may be different than today.

The key question to keep in mind is, "How can I serve my wife in a way that is honoring to the Lord and loving to her?"

BE EMOTIONALLY PRESENT WITH ENCOURAGEMENT

The words that we use have such a huge impact on our wives, for good or ill. You may not realize it, but the words you say (or don't say) to her on a daily basis have more influence than any other person's words. If you don't believe me, observe the effects that your kind words and compliments have on your wife. Watch her body language and pay attention to her overall demeanor—not just the immediate response (though that is tangible too) but the response over a period of time.

Our words to our wife are like nutrients absorbed by plants as they grow. I am reminded of this as I look out my back door. The neighbor who lives behind me has a beautiful yard. Their grass is green and thick with nary a weed anywhere. They fertilize and do all of the things needed to have a great yard and it is evident that they have been consistently doing so for years. My yard, however, is quite different. I mow and put a little fertilizer and weed killer down each year, but I do not spend the time and energy necessary to have a beautiful lawn—and it shows. There is a clear demarcation point between our two lawns, observable based on the health of the grass. In the same way, it is observable when we speak well to our wife, encouraging her and praising her. The effect becomes even more obvious over time.

Our words as a husband need to be filled with grace. Proverbs 16:24 says, "Gracious words are like a honeycomb, sweetness to the soul and health to the body." Proverbs 15:26 says, "The thoughts of the wicked are an abomination to the Lord, but gracious words are pure." Paul in his letter to the Ephesian church says, "Let no corrupting talk come out of your mouths, but only such as is good for building up, as fits the occasion, that it may give grace to those who hear" (Ephesians 4:29). Words are powerful, so we need to be cognizant of how we use them and make sure we control our tongue. James warns of the dangers of our mouths, that they are a "restless evil, full of deadly poison" (James 3:8b).

So, how do we use our words for good? First, start by telling your wife that you love her. Verbally utter those words so she hears them. Write it down on notes for her to see. It is easy to think our actions show our love, and they can, but it is equally important that she hear us say it.

Second, tell your wife that she is beautiful. Same thing—say it, write it, make it known repeatedly. She is made in the image of God and is precious in His sight, so remind her of this beauty. The world wants to absolutely destroy her and tell her she is only worthy if she looks a specific way, dresses a specific way, acts a specific way, and adorns herself in a specific way. The women in our culture are killing themselves as they try to achieve a false reality of perfection that can only be found in a CGI image after it has been altered. Adore her with the truth of her beauty.

Our Father tells us of His love for us and shows it in many ways. Let's do the same for our wife. Go kiss your wife and whisper, "I love you." Tell her what you admire about her beauty. Remember, speak truth to her. Do not lie to her by saying you like something when you really don't. It is not healthy and will cause more harm than good. Your compliments do not need to be lengthy or elaborate because at its root, a compliment tells your wife that you notice her and you are paying attention to her. When she wears a color you like, tell her she looks good in that color. If you like the way your wife styles her hair, tell her so. If she does something which really helps you, thank her and let her know how much you appreciate her. If you see her being a fantastic mom, point that out to her. *The key is to observe.* Above all, hold fast to the one the Lord gave you as a companion. She is the most important person to you on this earth, so let your words and actions extol her worth.

QUICK HITS FROM THE CHAPTER

- Spending intentional time with your wife is critical—not simply the quality of the time spent, but also the quantity of time.

- As a husband, we need to be emotionally engaged with our wife. We can do this by putting away all distractions (including our watch and phone) and listening to what our wife says and how she says it. Our job is not to fix things, but simply to listen.

- Tell your wife, "I love you" and "You are beautiful" at least once a day. Look for ways to verbally encourage her and praise her.

- What we do around the house and how we use our words will have a huge impact on our wives.

QUESTIONS FOR REFLECTION

1. How do you spend intentional time with your wife?

2. When was the last time you sat down with your wife and listened to her? Do you do this frequently, occasionally, or rarely?

3. In what ways would your wife like you to spend intentional time with her? If you do not know, sit down with her today and ask.

4. Which is harder for you: intentional time with your wife, being emotionally engaged around the house, or verbally encouraging your wife? What one action step can you take today to improve in that area?

CHAPTER 6

Be Intentional with your Children

We have discussed being intentional with our wife, so now let's look at being intentional with our children. Don't have kids? Do NOT skip this section! If you do not have children yet but would like to have children in the future, this is a good opportunity to begin thinking about this important skill. If you think you may never have children or do not want children, I still encourage you to read this chapter. As Christians, we are called to share the love of Christ with the world, and that includes children. You can pour into a niece or nephew, the child of the single-parent who lives next door, your co-worker's children, or even the youth at your church.

Also, assume that each child (if you have more than one) is different. They do not all like to do the same activities and are not all interested in the same things. If you were not previously aware of this, consider yourself made aware.

If you do not know your child's interests or what makes them tick—those things that bring them joy or make them feel special—have no fear, you can learn.

One way to learn this is through observation. What do they like most or what do they spend most of their free time doing? It may sound like a silly question, but we need to step back and assume we do not know this. I messed this up when I assumed my children all liked the same things. For example, all three of my children like to read (some more than others). However, they all like different kinds of books (subject, genre, style). The same goes for movies, activities, and food.

As you know by now, I am a book and movie geek, so of course I introduced my children to Tolkein's *The Lord of the Rings* trilogy, which should also not surprise you since I referenced it earlier in the book. I started reading the trilogy with my daughters and received mixed results. My older daughter finished the series on her own and has read them more than once. My younger daughter lost interest toward the end of the first book and we did not finish it—although she did enjoy watching the movies with me.

The second way to learn what your child likes is to ask them. It is important to remember though, your child will not always tell you what is true for them, but instead may tell you what they think you want to hear. In fact, it is very possible that your children (and spouse) simply humor you sometimes when they have absolutely no interest, desire, or affinity for the activity or subject. A father's approval and interest is so important to your children that they will frequently endure many struggles—even playing sports they do not like, instruments they loathe, activities they dread—simply because you like them. At the core, they do not want to disappoint you. Let that thought sink in for a moment. When we ask them what they would like to do together, we need to continue asking (graciously, gently) to confirm what is true. We do this though, *after* we have practiced observation.

I took piano lessons for several years when I was young and wish I had not stopped. My oldest daughter has played piano for several years and really enjoys it, gladly playing every day. My younger daughter played for a year, but did not have a great passion for it, and so we let her stop. My son has played for a couple years now and we are trying to decide whether he wants to continue or not. In each instance, my wife and I try to individually evaluate whether each child wants to play or not. As much as I would like for all of them to play, I do not want to force them.

Observing and asking are not the hardest part though. The third step is where things get real: we need to purposefully and intentionally do those activities with our children—and do them joyfully without sighs, eye rolling, phone checking, excuse making, and any other attitude that makes our child think we do not want to be there.

Begin today with the end result in mind. What do you want your children to say to you when they move out? "Thank you for listening to me and loving me when it was hard," or "Wahoo! I'm outta here!" You will not get many chances at this because if your children feel like you are dismissing them after they had the courage to be honest with you, they will tell you what you want to hear and then drift away. By the time they have some control over their time, they will look elsewhere to spend their time and you will have missed a great opportunity to build a relationship with them.

But take heart! Now is the day and now is the hour to act. Let's start by doing the following:

1.   Observe what your children like to do, read, or watch. Observe the things that draw their attention.

2.   Ask them about one of the things you observed. Ask with genuine curiosity as someone wanting to learn about it. They may not answer you, but keep trying.

3.   Listen to what they say and what they do not say. By what they do not say, I mean notice what their body language tells you. If you ask them if they like something and they say "yes," but their answer has no enthusiasm and their body language screams the opposite, maybe they are saying yes just to appease you.

4.   Don't give up. This is a marathon, not a sprint. Keep trying.

If your children are out of the house, it is not too late. Try to do these same steps with them based on your current situation.

TRY SOMETHING TOTALLY NEW

Sometimes just taking a risk and trying something new can be awesome. When we step out of our comfort zone, especially if it is something our children want to do, it can not only be fun, but it can provide long-term dividends in our lives. I struggle with this because I have serious perfectionistic tendencies stemming from my own sinful pride which sometimes limit me. The times when we can try something and then laugh at our own success/failure/ineptitude always places us in a different light with our children.

For example, a few years ago, I started baking with each of my two daughters when they were around nine and ten. I decided we needed to learn how to bake bread from scratch—yeast, flour, the whole thing. I had never used yeast in my life, so I was taking a risk. However, I trusted the instructions to guide us. I searched for a wheat bread recipe, went to the store to buy the ingredients, and then we tried to make the bread. It was a lot of fun. I only sort of knew what I was doing based on cooking shows I had watched and a little guesswork from my other cooking experiences. The bread turned out great, we enjoyed eating our creation, and made a point of baking it again.

A couple weeks later, I tracked down a family friend's yeast roll recipe that I knew was very good but seemed a bit overwhelming. We made the attempt and it turned out well too. I then started looking for other breads we might enjoy eating. We tried some that were great (we found an excellent and simple Italian bread recipe—check it out in the Vault of Books, Food, and Fun at the end of the book) and some that were not so good, but ultimately, we had fun and we connected.

Baking has become an activity that I regularly share with my daughters, and it's a constant opportunity to connect with them. What activity can you start with your child that can grow into a consistent avenue for connection? This works for children of any age too, but the key point is to pick something and try it. If it falls apart, don't worry about it, just pick something different next time—it's supposed to be fun, not a grade on a final exam.

DON'T JUST READ ABOUT IT—*DO SOMETHING!*

My son and I have become quite the swordsmen (using soft rubber swords, of course), and marksmen (shooting each other with soft spongy darts), and trampoline acrobats on our trampoline. Did you know that you can create two fun swords simply by cutting a pool noodle in half and wrapping tape around each end to mimic sword handles? See the full tutorial in the Vault of Books, Food, and Fun—hours of fun and you can play in the house.

I used to bounce on the trampoline with my daughters too, but they are older now, and no longer enjoy it. I am not a very outdoorsy kind of person and neither are my children, but that can be a way to connect with your kids if they enjoy nature. I find no pleasure in camping, but would be willing to camp if my children liked it. (By the way, many men love getting outside. But for people who do not like the outdoors, the act of camping can be miserable, so it is best to find out if your children like it first. Trust me on this one!)

Reading with your children can be a great experience too. Many studies show the positive benefits of parents reading to their children, not only during the pre-kindergarten years, but also from ages six and beyond.[7] Some of the benefits include improved listening skills, reading comprehension, vocabulary, and literacy skills.[8] Find something your children like to read and go through it together. It gives you a common experience and talking points, while also allowing for a wide-range of conversations about life. You can talk about good and evil, history, humor, what life was like for you when you were younger, and so many other topics. I read with my children individually and together, and the books range the gamut of styles and genres. (For a list of my book suggestions, see the Vault of Books, Food, and Fun.)

Board games can be a neat way to spend time and make memories together too. Pick one night a week and commit to playing a game that your children select. Our family favorites include Go Fish and Rummy, along with many classic board games.

I highly recommend taking your children out on a date or out for a fun time. This is especially true for dads and daughters. With my son, we just go out—no date. This does not have to be expensive—definitely make it budget-friendly. When my daughters were really young (two or three) and we had no money, I would take them individually to Walmart, look at toys, and get a cupcake from the Walmart bakery. It was just an opportunity to spend some fun time together.

In the last few years, I made it a point to take each of my kids out to eat and then do some type of special activity about once a quarter. Sometimes we would just go to the bookstore and look around, or go paint pottery, or go indoor rock climbing, or anything else that sounded fun to them. With my son, we would usually go look at toys (he is eight now). He and I used to go to Home Depot or Lowe's to look at tools and such, which was fun for both of us.

The most important part of this whole process is to spend time together because we learn by what we observe. This is especially true with fathers and sons. When I was in middle school, my Dad and I went hunting each November during deer season. I never shot a deer, but looking back on it now, that was not important. What mattered was the time spent together, just learning and observing as sons do with their fathers. I learned what it meant to sacrifice for my family and to do what was needed even when it was hard.

The list can be infinite, but the main thing is to start doing something. What's one thing you can do to spend intentional time with your kids this week? Block out thirty minutes or an hour on your calendar to ensure that it happens.

BE EMOTIONALLY PRESENT
WITH ENCOURAGEMENT

Remember what I said about encouraging our wives? You guessed it! The same concept applies with our children. Think back to your childhood for a moment and recall a time when someone praised or encouraged you. Now, think back to a time when someone did the opposite. Just in your own mind, without telling anyone else, how did you feel? Did you notice any difference between the two?

With those memories fixed firmly in the front of our minds, what do we need to do as fathers? Start by telling your children that you love them. Say the words out loud and write the words on paper, white boards, chalkboards, texts—pick a medium they like and write it down. Our children need to hear and see our love. You might be thinking, "They know I love them. I don't have to say it." Are you sure? Make sure there are no doubts!

If you have children, remember, they are your disciples. You may not think of them that way, but they are. This is not a new idea I came up with—it is found throughout Scripture. We are commanded in Matthew 28:19-20 to make disciples, and we will have the greatest influence on the disciples in our own home. As our children grow up, they will see what it means to be a husband and father by our example. We cannot outsource this to our wives, the Church, or anyone else. We must remind them, tell them, show them, and teach them with actions and words what it means to follow Christ. They are made in the image of God and He has entrusted them to us. The world wants to corrupt and destroy them, and so it is important that our children hear encouragement and love from us. They need to observe us living as a godly man, husband, and father.

If you have daughters, praise their beauty. Being beautiful does not require being dressed up in preparation to go out with friends, nor does it mean that their hair and makeup (if they use makeup) are perfect. No, they are beautiful because they are not only made in the image of God, but they are beautiful because they are made by God as His creation. Our daughters are unique, talented, delightful, and beautiful because of *who they are and not what they look like or what they can do.* Remind her of her beauty each day because chances are she may doubt her own value and worth each time she looks in the mirror. She will see a small blemish and miss the radiant smile that lights up a room. She may hate her hair and ignore her eyes which sparkle with joy and delight. Compliments might frequently bounce off of her and not be accepted while the merest slight (real or perceived) will be absorbed and digested like food. She needs to hear her father praise her beauty because, believe it or not, what we think matters to her.

It is also important that our children hear us say the words, "I am proud of you." Use this in the context of effort and work, not based on the results of that work. We should pursue excellence, but excellence comes through consistent effort and work.

For example, if your child plays a sport, praise their work ethic and sportsmanship regardless of the scoreboard at the end of the game. If they consistently put in the time and effort, then it is praiseworthy. Scoreboards can be fickle, so we need to be careful not to praise them for victories only. If we do, our kids will think they are only acceptable and valuable to us if they win. The same idea applies to music, dance, theater, writing, academics, or any other activity in which they participate. Remember, your kids will work hard to hear the words, "I am proud of you." Let's influence them towards actions that have the most worth.

Okay, time to act. Go hug your son and tell him, "I love you." Go take your daughter by the hand and sing, "I love you." Say it aloud to them, looking them in the eyes so they know you mean it. Look for ways to say, "I am proud of you."

WHEN CHILDREN LEAVE HOME

LifeWay recently conducted a study on college students and their church attendance.[9] They found that two-thirds of college students who attended a Protestant church regularly during their teenage years for a least a year, dropped out for at least a year when they reached college. The study listed various reasons for their dropping out, but the bottom line was these students did not think it was important enough to join a local church and be involved in the work of Christ.

My heart broke when I read this. I grieve over it. Granted, these are adults who are now responsible for their own decisions. We cannot provide salvation for our children—only Jesus can do that. All we can do is model what it means to follow the Lord, pray diligently for our children, and trust that the Lord is in control.

Do you know what grieves me the most? These students learned about the importance of Christ and being a part of His work from their parents, especially their fathers. If the students did not think the local church was relevant to their lives, many would have seen that demonstrated at home—either by their lack of a faithful walk with the Lord or by the church environment where their family worshipped.

Remember, we reap what we sow. We cannot expect apples if we plant orange seeds and we cannot expect our children to pursue Jesus if we do not pursue Him and hold Him high.

If our churches are not biblically sound and we still insist on being a part of that local body of believers, what result can we expect from our children? If the gospel and the Bible are not relevant in our churches, if obedience to Christ is only for "really good" Christians, if community within the church is ignored, if commitment to the local church is a punchline, then this falling away is to be expected.

Unfortunately, even if we pursue Jesus diligently, model walking with Him faithfully, disciple our children consistently, bring our families to solid churches, and serve gladly within those churches, our children can still walk away from the faith. I recently spoke with a man whom I greatly respect. He is a godly man who is faithful in his walk with Christ and who has made sure his family has been a part of a sound church. He has done all of the things Scripture calls husbands and fathers to do, yet one of his children (now in their early twenties) has turned from God and is running in the opposite direction.

Being faithful to Jesus does not mean our children will be faithful to Him. I tremble as I write these words. My children are still at home (the oldest are in middle school), but I look ahead to when they move away and must claim their faith as their own. All I can do is be faithful in my walk with Christ and help them do the same. It is my goal to do all I can.

When you imagine your children's future, what do you envision? Do your desires for them only revolve around successful careers and long life, or do you want each of your children to pursue items of eternal consequence? Are you leading them toward a faithful relationship with the Lord and an investment in a Christ-like church community? If not, what can you change right now to foster that possibility? We cannot predict the future or manipulate our kids to do as we please, but we can proactively disciple them while they live at home.

QUICK HITS FROM THE CHAPTER

- Spend time doing things with your children that they enjoy, even if you are not good at the activity.

- Each day, tell your children, "I love you." Make it a point to tell your daughters, "You are beautiful." Observe ways to encourage your children and tell them, "I am proud of you."

- What we do and how we engage with our children will have a direct impact on how they live once they leave home. We have a limited amount of time to influence and guide them.

QUESTIONS FOR REFLECTION

1. How do you spend intentional time with your child(ren)?

2. If you do not have children yet and hope to have them in the future, what is one way you would spend intentional time with them?

3. What is one activity that you could do this week with your child(ren) that they would enjoy?

4. Do you say the words, "I love you," to each of your child(ren)? If not, how can you begin saying this to them? If so, do you say it to them daily?

5. When you praise your child(ren), what behaviors are you encouraging? Are you concerned more with their success or with their work ethic? What is one area or quality you can praise your child(ren) for this week?

CHAPTER 7

Be Intentional with Spiritual Matters

We have covered a lot of ground together. We have talked through some everyday means of leading well and spending time effectively with our families. Now let's talk through something even more important: being intentional with spiritual matters. Husbands and fathers—this is on us.

Unfortunately, too often husbands and fathers do not do this. Even I am guilty of this. We assume the church is there to teach our children about the Bible and how to follow Christ. Or we let our wives lead this function in our homes. I think part of the issue is fear—fear of not knowing the answers, fear of failure, fear of stepping up and being responsible, fear of ridicule among family, friends, business associates, and culture.

Fear is real, but it is not the end. The Lord told Joshua to be strong and courageous three different times in the first chapter of the book of Joshua when he was preparing to lead the people into the Promised Land. Joshua would not have needed such encouragement if he were not feeling afraid.

Before David died, he encouraged his son Solomon regarding the building of the Temple, "Be strong and courageous and do it. Do not be afraid and do not be dismayed, for the Lord God, even my God, is with you. He will not leave you or forsake you, until all the work for the service of the house of the Lord is finished" (1 Chronicles 28:20). Solomon would not have needed a reminder if fear were not present.

David again wrote in Psalm 56, praying to the Lord, "Be gracious to me, O God, for man tramples on me; all day long an attacker oppresses me; my enemies trample on me all day long, for many attack me proudly. When I am afraid, I put my trust in you. In God, whose word I praise, in God I trust; I shall not be afraid. What can flesh do to me?" (Psalm 56:1-4). David does not say he has no fear, but that when he is afraid he looks to the Lord, trusting in Him, because only through the Lord can the fear subside.

So let's be men like David who acknowledge our fear. And let's use our fears as an opportunity to trust in the Lord. He will encourage us in the same ways He encouraged Joshua and David and Solomon. I desperately need to hear David's words in this Psalm because I am afraid every day. I need to say them aloud, cry out to the Lord, and ask Him to help me put one foot in front of the other in spite of the fear. My strength is small, but the Lord is bigger than anything I will face. The Lord will not leave us alone in our fear. He is here to help us walk through it.

GATHERING AT CHURCH FOR WORSHIP

Where to begin though? Let's start with the church gathering. Robbie Low describes a Swiss survey conducted in the mid-1990's to see if a person's religion carried from one generation to another and if so, why. The results were rather amazing.

He said the survey found that the father had the greatest influence on whether his children became regular worshippers, and by quite a significant amount. If a father never attended a worship service, then there was a two percent chance that his children would later attend regularly. If a father attended a worship service regularly (once a week), there was at least a 66% chance his children would attend regularly. Low concluded that Scripture points out the importance of the father and human behavior agrees.[10]

Our job as husbands and fathers is to make sure that we bring our families to worship the Lord with other people on a weekly basis. It is not my wife's responsibility to do this, nor is it my children's responsibility to want to go. It is on us, and if we have things in our life that consistently prevent this from happening, we need to step back and find out how we can reorient our lives to make church a priority.

Do we have activities that get in the way or are our children in so many activities that it prevents us from being able to go to a weekly service? If so, we need to prayerfully evaluate what needs to change.

If we work on Sunday mornings, we need to find a church that has an evening service, or a service on a different day and time during the week. For example, there are churches in the city where I live that have Thursday and Saturday evening services to try to reach those people who cannot make it on Sunday. If we cannot find such a church, we need to pray earnestly for an opportunity to work at a different place so that we can worship together at a local church. Yes, it really is that important.

At the end of the day, our walk with Christ and our responsibility to biblically lead our wives and children are of greatest importance—far more than anything this world suggests is more valuable.

Now, is it okay to miss church on a weekend? Yes. Does sickness prevent it? Yes, and if you or your family are sick, please stay home and do not share your germs. Does travel prevent it sometimes? Yes. I am not saying salvation is based on being at a church service fifty-two weeks each year. What I am saying is that we cannot grow if we are not involved in a church.

What's holding you back? Fear? Anxiety? Let's practice what we just read about in Psalm 56 by calling out to the Lord and saying, "Lord, I am afraid! Help me to follow you and be obedient to you!"

Next, decide right now, before you read any further, to find a worship service to attend this week and share these thoughts with your wife. If you are friends with other Christ-followers, call or text them and ask where they worship. We will look at what to look for in a church in this next section, but resolve to attend one church service this week.

WHAT IF YOU ARE NOT CURRENTLY PART OF A CHURCH?

You might have read the last section, decided that you need to take action, but then do not know where to go. You may not currently be a part of a church or feel connected to any one church body. You might also be in the process of moving or have recently moved to a new area. How do you determine which church to attend?

This is important because not all churches are created equal. I do not mean things like size, shape, worship style, dress, parking, or website. Those can be helpful and do affect our desire to be a part of it, but in many ways those items come down to personal taste and preference. We can worship Christ in an old building or a new building or no building at all. In saying not all churches are created equal, I mean not all churches believe and teach the same things.

I have narrowed down this list to things which are foundational to Christianity, meaning if a church does not teach and believe this, they are not following Christ. I encourage you to read this list and look up the verse references for yourself. If you are not sure how to do this, take heart and do not be afraid! At the front of the Bible, there is a table of contents and page numbers to guide you. If you use an electronic or online Bible, just key the reference into the search function. This is a great way to practice evaluating the Biblical validity of someone's teaching.

Look for a church that proclaims the following theological beliefs:

THE BIBLE

The 66 books of the Old and New Testaments are God's complete, verbally inspired revelation to us. The original texts were written without error in their original languages and are the ultimate authority for faith in Christ, living as a follower of Christ, and for the Church. See Psalm 119:160; 2 Timothy 3:16-17; 2 Peter 1:20-21.

GOD

There is one God who has no beginning and no end. He is the creator and sustainer of all things. He is one God who exists eternally in three persons: Father, Son, and Holy Spirit. He is sinless. See Genesis 1-2; Deuteronomy 6:4; Psalm 90:2; Matthew 28:19; John 1:1, 14; John 4:24; Colossians 1:15-19.

JESUS

Jesus Christ is fully man and fully God and is the second person of the Trinity. He was conceived by the Holy Spirit, born of a virgin, and lived a sinless life. He allowed Himself to be betrayed and killed by sinful men, was buried for three days, was resurrected on the third day, appeared to over 500 people after He was resurrected, and ascended into heaven to the right hand of the Father from where He will one day return. See Matthew 1:18-23; 1 Corinthians 15; Philippians 2:5-11; 1 Thessalonians 4:14-17; 1 Timothy 2:5-6; Revelation 19:11-16.

PEOPLE

People (men and women, you and I) are made in the image of God. We are not God—we are His creation. When Adam and Eve came into the world, they were without sin, but when they disobeyed God, they became sinful and separated from God. All descendants from them (all people, including you and I) are born with sinful natures and willingly sin against God. We cannot fix our sin on our own. Every part of our being is affected by sin. See Genesis 1:27-28; Genesis 2:7-3:24; Psalm 8:4-8, 51:5; John 3:19-21; Romans 3:9-26; 1 John 1:8-10.

SALVATION

Salvation only comes through faith in the shed blood of Jesus Christ for the forgiveness of our sins. Through faith in Christ alone, we are justified before God and sealed with the Holy Spirit as a guarantee of our inheritance, which is eternal life with Christ in heaven. See John 3:16-18; Romans 5:1, 10:9-13; Galatians 2:20-21; Philippians 1:6, 3:20-21; Ephesians 2:8-10; 1 John 1:9, 2:2.

These are the major points, and I only want to major on the majors. As followers of Christ, we may disagree on some other topics, but the elements listed above are critical.

Check your church's core belief statements (they are likely listed on their website or available in the church). See if these things are listed. You will likely find additional items listed as well, and that is okay because they tell you about how the church functions and how it handles things like baptism and communion. Again, I am not addressing that here.

Once you find out if the church holds to these things, listen to a few sermons and evaluate what they are actually saying. Most churches have links to previous sermons on their website. As you read your Bible and grow in your walk with the Lord, compare what they are teaching with what the Bible says.

When we moved to Tennessee six years ago, finding a home church was critical. I started by taking inventory of people I knew who were followers of Christ and who previously lived in the area. In this instance, I reached out to a friend who fit that criteria and asked for suggestions about churches. He gave me some great insight about a particular church. I looked at that church's website to see what they believed. I read their doctrinal or belief statement to see if they were sound. They sounded fantastic, and the sermons were in alignment too.

My family and I visited that church a few times. We observed the people in the congregation, the staff, and the pastors. We looked at material sent home from our children's classes to see what they were being taught. We attended a new members lunch to meet the two teaching pastors and to learn what the church was about and how it functioned. During the church worship service, we compared the sermon with Scripture, to make sure the teaching aligned with scripture. After a few weeks of this, we knew this was a solid church that taught God's Word and we wanted to be a part of it.

After reading this, you are probably ready to yell at me and say, "Eric, that sounds like a lot of hard work just to find a church! You are taking this way too seriously! Do I really need to do this?" Maybe you are more subdued and would not come right out and yell at me—but you are likely thinking it nonetheless. I will answer you with a question: How much due diligence would you take when buying a house?

While house hunting, you visit the house at least two or three times before making an offer (not counting the times you drive around the neighborhood). You ask your realtor what they think of the house and what they see in it because they have expertise, experience. and knowledge—not only of houses in general, but of this market specifically.

Once you make an offer and the seller accepts it, you order a home inspection to tell you if the house is structurally sound and if any problems exist. If the inspection uncovers serious issues, you have the opportunity to ask the seller to fix those problems or you can rescind your offer. If the inspection does not identify any major complications, you gain additional confidence that the house is sound. After four to eight weeks of due diligence and work on your part, you close on your new house and receive the keys.

There are other steps in the home-buying process which I did not mention, like a termite inspection or a survey. The key point is this—if you are willing to spend this much time (and money) to make sure the house is sound before you buy it, would you not be willing to do the same amount of due diligence to find out if a church is sound? A house shapes the environment in which our family lives. How much more does a church shape and influence our families for eternity?

It is an important process and we must be responsible for initiating it. Now is a great time to start this journey. If you already attend a church, why not remind yourself of the core mission statements that your body believes? Look on their website and see what they proclaim as true. Look up the verses that reference their belief statements. Do they fit with what you read above? What other statements do they include? Can you find Biblical support for those statements?

FINDING BIBLICAL COMMUNITY

Biblical community is step two in the journey. You may or may not be familiar with that term, but it essentially means a church group, small group, bible study, or anything else that puts you in the midst of other Christ followers so that you can grow in Christ. Biblical community allows you to ask questions of those people who are farther along in life and who have gone through the challenges you now face. It allows you to ask questions of those families who are going through the same life stage as you. You can share your struggles and celebrate victories with them and they can do likewise with you, all the while praying for each other and encouraging one another.

As a very private person who struggles with pride, biblical community does not come easily to me. I have found though, that asking for help from these like-minded people and sharing life with them makes all the difference in the world. My wife and I lead a small group that meets in our home every two weeks. I like to say our group is a true picture of the church because it represents the entire demographic spectrum, from ages nineteen to late sixties and every decade in-between. As we talk and share with one another, I am reminded that I am not alone in this walk. I see how the men older than me have made decisions with their families and in their faith walk, and can use them as a reference for similar situations which I will face. My wife and I have been married for twenty years, so we have been able to encourage those who have only been married a few years. We have even been a resource for them in parenting. In addition, our children watch us seeking biblical community, and we hope it helps them realize the importance of it and motivates each of them to pursue it as well.

If you don't currently have a biblical community around you, now is a great time to start. I remember feeling so overwhelmed when we first started going to our church. We were new to the state, did not know anyone, and we felt so isolated and alone. I knew we needed community. I especially knew my wife needed to connect with other women and our children needed to connect with other children in a biblical context. Thankfully, our church had a way to sign up for small groups and we were able to get started.

Relationships do not develop overnight, but they must start somewhere. Ask your church leaders about opportunities to join a bible study. Sign up for the next men's study or prayer event. Invite a few men from your body to gather together one morning a week for prayer. Community doesn't look perfect, but it does look like believers gathering together to love, encourage, and pray for one another.

SERVING IN THE LOCAL CHURCH

The next step is to make sure we are not only bringing our families *to* a church, but that we are committed to being involved at the church through serving. To be a follower of Christ is to serve His church and to be a blessing to other believers. One of the reasons we find so many "one another" verses in the Bible is that we are gifted by the Holy Spirit to serve one another.

There are a myriad of ways that we can serve in the local church, so ask one of the pastors, elders, or staff members at your church how you can use your talents to fill a need. You might be asking, "How do I know what to do?" A mentor once shared with me a great way to find a place to serve that fits you: if there is a need, serve there. Try it for six months and see if the Lord has gifted you for it or if you have a desire to serve there. If it works well, that is great! Continue serving there. If not, that is okay—you learned something. Look around for another need and serve there for six months and follow the same pattern until you find a place where you fit well. It is a bonus if you and your wife can serve together!

Serving will influence your wife and children as you lead by example. Not only that, but we are called to serve. If you are a follower of Christ, you are to serve His body. No exceptions. If you are not serving in some capacity as you read this, mark your place in this book, set it down, and reach out to a leader at your church, someone in your small group, or a Sunday School teacher to find out how you can begin serving.

LEADING YOUR FAMILY IN BIBLE STUDY/DEVOTIONS

Now that we are committed to bringing our families to a local church gathering and being involved in that church, let's talk about what we can do at home. Husbands and fathers can lead family devotions and teach our families the Bible—even if your wife also teaches your children. However, I know that such a task can feel daunting and overwhelming. Where do we begin and how do we make it work?

This fear of failure can keep us from trying or to quit once we have tried something a few times because it is scary and we do not know if we are doing it right. Sometimes, we let our wives handle it because they may seem more spiritually advanced than us or we think they are better at teaching our children. Let me share a very hard truth: our wives can have advanced degrees in theology and biblical languages or have spent years as a missionary in a foreign country, but ultimately we must take responsibility for this. This doesn't diminish our wife's intelligence or experience. It's simply the way God has defined our roles.

If you have younger children, one of the easiest ways to start is to get a children's Bible like *The Gospel Story Bible* by Marty Machowski and A. E. Macha, *The Jesus Storybook Bible* by Sally Lloyd-Jones and Jago, or *The Big Picture Story Bible* by David Helm and Gail Schoonmaker. I have used each of these over the years and they are great for teaching your children basic bible truth and the overarching, unified scope of the Bible from Genesis to Revelation.

When my kids were younger, we would sit down before they went to sleep at night, read a chapter from one of these Bibles, and talk about it. When we reached the end of the book, we would read it again. We have gone through these Bibles several times each, and though it may seem overblown, the purpose is to get them immersed in the biblical narrative and help them see how it all fits together. It also shows them the importance of having Bible study as part of a daily routine.

But my kids aren't so little anymore, so something else that we have started using lately is systematic theology books. Wait...you do what? Yes, we talk through theology too, and it is as needed for me as it is for them. One book I would recommend is *Big Truths for Young Hearts* by Bruce Ware. I suggest starting this when your kids are in sixth or seventh grade, but my son (eight years old) has also listened as we have read through it. The idea is to help them (and yourself) see overarching truths of the faith.

We have also started reading missionary biographies. I have purchased a few from YWAM Publishing as well as some other sources. They are inspirational because they provide a view into the lives of believers who have gone before us and they also open our eyes to a larger world where the gospel is desperately needed.

Books are helpful resources, but we have read through various books in the Bible as well. We recently read through the four gospels and Acts. It was a great time of questions and discussion and learning for all of us. Remember, you don't have to have all the answers. Write down the questions that come up and research them or ask someone who can help you answer those questions. If your children are old enough, assign questions for them to research and have them report back to the family.

If you're not sure where to start, check out my recommended books in the Vault of Books, Food, and Fun. Pick one, purchase it, and start a daily habit with your family.

PRAYING WITH YOUR FAMILY

Do you pray with your family apart from the dinner table? Praying with our families can be as intimidating as leading them in Bible study. If you're like me, you've probably thought, "What do I pray and how do I say it?"

There are many guides/methods to prayer, but one that I find effective is the ACTS method:

- Adoration: praising God for who He is. You could say, "Lord, You are good. You made heaven and earth and everything in it. You are trustworthy and true and perfect in every way."

- Confession: acknowledging our sins to God and agreeing with God that we have sinned. You could pray, "Lord, I sinned against you. I let my anger flare up when I responded to my wife and I snapped at her. My attitude has been horrible lately and I have not been thankful for anything. Please forgive me, Lord. Help me to walk with You and change my heart."

- Thanksgiving: thanking the Lord for who He is and what He has done. You could say, "Lord, thank you for saving me from my sin and redeeming me. Thank you for my job and my family because both are from Your hands. Thank You Lord that You are in control even when things seem out of control. I can trust in You."

- Supplication: asking the Lord for what is on our heart. This is usually what we think of when we hear prayer.

This is not a be-all-end-all method and it is not necessary to follow this pattern every time, but it can definitely keep us on track. Plus, it provides a framework not only to pray at that moment, but also to teach our children.

You can also sit down with the Bible and pray through scripture. For example, you can start at the beginning of Romans chapter eight, read it aloud, then pray through it like this. "Lord, thank you that there is no condemnation for those in Christ, that you have set me free from sin and death, free from condemnation, all because of what Christ did on the cross. Help us to remember it, rest in it, and live like it tomorrow as we go to work and school. Remind us Lord, that we are yours." I recommend this pattern of prayer after you read and discuss the bible with your children.

Additionally, you can pray for:

- People who do not know Christ - that they would put their faith in Christ and follow Him.
- Countries and people groups around the world, asking that those people would hear the gospel, become a disciple of Christ, be discipled, and make disciples.
- Believers around the globe who are going through intense and severe persecution.
- Your church and the work it is doing.
- Your pastors and elders, your teachers and greeters, your staff and students.

It is always a good idea to ask your wife and kids what they want to pray for. When you sit down with them to have a devotional time, ask them how you can pray for what is on their hearts and minds. You may only get silence from them at this question for a day or a month or longer, but that is okay. Keep asking and as they see you pray, they will begin sharing.

GIVING WITH YOUR FAMILY

We discussed challenges with money in an earlier chapter, so we will not review that topic here. Instead, we will examine the act of giving, especially within the context of home. You may have mastered this particular area or you may not think at all about giving. Regardless of where you land on the spectrum, let's examine what biblical giving looks like and how to model it within our families.

Biblical offering goes all the way back to Genesis 4 where we see Cain and Abel make offerings to the Lord, and it continues all the way through the New Testament. From a biblical viewpoint, giving does a few things:

1. It is an act of worship to the Lord. As we give of our finances, we are acknowledging that the Lord will provide for our needs. I am paid every two weeks, and when I am paid, my wife and I will sit down and balance our checkbook, go through our budget, and pay our bills. The first item we pay is a tithe to our local church. We give a minimum of ten percent of our gross income. A tithe really equals ten percent, but I am using the term to denote the first gift to the church, which is at least ten percent. It is not always easy, but we do it as an act of worship, acknowledging that the Lord is the provider of all that we have (life, food, home, family, income, etc.), and so we give to Him and His work. This money does not go to a unique ministry or a service organization—those are great things to support, but the first percentage of our money goes directly to the local church where we worship. We also

give other monies to missions or ministries on a regular or one-time basis as needs appear. Our family would call those "offerings".

2. We teach our children the act of giving. They see us give regularly in worship to our church, to missions, and to those in need. With the money they earn, they put ten percent towards giving. At this point, we are letting them decide what ministry they would like to support. They collect it in a container until they decide where to give it. They have given money to support orphanages and to an organization that teaches Bible studies to children. They have given to international Bible translation projects, agriculture organizations who provide animals for families to raise as a source of income, and to homeless relief.

3. Our giving supports the work of God's kingdom here on earth. The Lord uses us to do work on earth and He uses the money He has given to us to do His work. This is one way He allows us to be involved in the process.

In 2 Corinthians 8, we see Paul writing to the Corinthian church about the generosity of the Macedonians,

> For in a severe test of affliction, their abundance of joy and their extreme poverty have overflowed in a wealth of generosity on their part. For they gave according to their means, as I can testify, and beyond their means, of their own accord, begging us earnestly for the favor of taking part in the relief of the saints—and this, not as we expected, but they gave themselves first to the Lord and then by the will of God to us (2 Corinthians 8:2-5).

Two things jump out in this text. First, they were in extreme poverty and yet they had an abundance of joy. Circumstances did not affect their joy or their desire to give. Second, they gave to those in need in Jerusalem after they gave themselves first to the Lord. These believers sought the Lord and rested in His grace and provision. In response to their time with the Lord, they gave sacrificially and joyfully.

Does that convict you? It convicts me! I do not always give joyfully, but out of obedience and faith. I also give when I see needs that need to be met, but sometimes it is hard. I frequently have to confess to the Lord and ask for forgiveness for my selfishness. Then I try to thank Him for all that He has given to me. "Help me, Lord, to gladly give as much as you want to whomever you want because you have lavished your grace and blessings upon me, one who has no merit in your eyes apart from Christ's righteousness."

If we jump to 2 Corinthians 9, Paul is talking with the Corinthians about their own giving in light of the Macedonian's giving. Paul knows the Corinthians have committed themselves to giving, but he also knows that sometimes commitments made are not always commitments fulfilled. He writes:

> The point is this: whoever sows sparingly will also reap sparingly, and whoever sows bountifully will also reap bountifully. Each one must give as he has decided in his heart, not reluctantly or under compulsion, for God loves a cheerful giver. And God is able to make all grace abound to you, so that having all sufficiency in all things at all times, you may abound in every good work. As it is written, "He has distributed freely, he has given to the poor; his righteousness endures forever." He who supplies seed to the sower and bread for food will supply and multiply your seed for sowing and increase the harvest of your righteousness. You will be enriched in every way to

be generous in every way, which through us will produce thanksgiving to God (2 Corinthians 9:6-11).

Paul makes it clear that giving needs to be joyful, not reluctant or under compulsion. He also proclaims that God will provide. If you are fearful of giving because you think there is not enough in the budget to give to God *and* your bills, Paul tells you to trust the One who supplies it all. If Jesus can take five small loaves and two fish to feed over 5000 people, if God can create the universe out of nothing by simply speaking, then He can provide what we need if we seek Him, worship Him, and rest in Him.

We are once again talking about sowing and reaping—you get what you plant. Please understand something though, and this is very important. If you give an amount of money to the Lord, it does not mean you will get more money in return. This is not "name it and claim it," and it is not the false prosperity gospel. The Lord says He will provide for you so you can be generous, and then there is a harvest of righteousness to be reaped from the love of Christ you have planted through your giving. The Lord says He will provide what you need, and what we actually need may be quite different than what we think we need. We always want to make sure we approach giving with humility because we are limited in our own understanding.

To bring it full circle with what we discussed in the beginning of chapter two: who is your God or god? If we pursue Christ, seek Him, and let the Holy Spirit work in us and through us, how we approach giving will be affected.

QUICK HITS FROM THE CHAPTER

- We need to lead our families in spiritual matters, starting with being a part of a local church.

- How we pursue Christ and serve Him will have a profound influence (whether for good or ill) on whether our families pursue Christ.

- Bible study, prayer, serving, giving—all of these serve as the basis for what we can teach our families.

- We do not have to know everything, but we do need to start somewhere.

- We are called to intentionally invite our families into prayer, study, and giving.

QUESTIONS FOR REFLECTION

1. How frequently do you initiate taking your family to a worship service on the weekends (or during the week if not on the weekends)?

2. How do you disciple your wife and children? What do you read together? How do you pray together? If you're not already doing this, where can you begin?

3. What spiritual seeds are you sowing in the lives of your wife and children based on your actions today? What kind of harvest will come from those seeds? What changes is the Lord telling you to make?

CHAPTER 8

Finishing Well

Have you ever flown before? I've learned that it does not matter how wonderfully you take off the runway or how smoothly the flight goes in the air, if the plane does not land properly, then the flight was not successful. (Thankfully all of my flights have been successful!)

Landing a plane physically and metaphorically is important. For example, you could hear an amazing sermon with memorable illustrations and challenging points, but all can be lost if they do not finish it well. You have probably heard at least one sermon in your life where the pastor kept speaking long after their key point was explained. They just needed to end it and call it a day. The message might have been excellent, but excellent ended ten minutes ago and now your thoughts are drifting.

Leading well as a husband and father is not only how we live each day during mid-flight, but also how we prepare for the future "landing." As followers of Christ, we look ahead to that day when we will be with Christ—even though we all carry some fear or uneasiness about actually dying. Paul writes in 2 Corinthians regarding this:

For we know that if the tent that is our earthly home is destroyed, we have a building from God, a house not made with hands, eternal in the heavens. For in this tent we groan, longing to put on our heavenly dwelling, if indeed by putting it on we may not be found naked. For while we are still in this tent, we groan, being burdened—not that we would be unclothed, but that we would be further clothed, so that what is mortal may be swallowed up by life. He who has prepared us for this very thing is God, who has given us the Spirit as a guarantee. So we are always of good courage. We know that while we are at home in the body we are away from the Lord, for we walk by faith, not by sight. Yes, we are of good courage, and we would rather be away from the body and at home with the Lord. So whether we are at home or away, we make it our aim to please him. For we must all appear before the judgment seat of Christ, so that each one may receive what is due for what he has done in the body, whether good or evil (2 Corinthians 5:1-10).

Paul is pointing out that life here on earth is temporary, but that we have an eternal home which cannot be taken away. In fact, we have an internal desire to be free of the pain and sorrow of life on earth as we look ahead to the joy of heaven. Don't you long for the day when you won't have to watch your kids fall and get hurt, or for the place where your wife can no longer cry tears of sadness on your shoulder? The Holy Spirit is the guarantee of our membership in heaven, and we are to walk faithfully until that day comes.

Our daily focus is to please the Lord through our faith, love, and obedience to Him, and we will be rewarded for this faith. If we pursue Christ in this way—eyes on the future while living faithfully now—then let's also lead our families with the same vision and purpose as we follow Christ. But what happens to our family after we go to heaven? Are they prepared for when we die?

WHAT HAPPENS IF WE DIE EARLIER THAN EXPECTED?

Are our families prepared for when we die? I do not mean emotionally prepared, because grief and loss will occur—though modeling what it means to follow Christ will help them not to grieve as those without hope (1 Thessalonians 4:13). If we die tomorrow, will our households be prepared so that our wives and children will be able to emotionally grieve for our loss without having to deal with the administrative stress of legal documents and other accounts?

This is where we need to lead courageously. It is easy to push this off saying, "It will be fine. I do not need to think of such things until I am older." The Lord knows how long we will live and has known it since He created the heavens and the earth. Nothing we can do will thwart His plan or cause that day to deviate from when it was originally decided. Here's the thing— the Lord has not told me when my last day will occur, and I am reasonably confident that the Lord has not told you either. As much as we might think we will live to eighty or ninety, we are not guaranteed anything beyond this moment. To assume otherwise is to liken ourselves to the rich fool in Jesus' parable found in Luke 12:13-21, who was so focused on himself and his wealth that he was not generous, ignored the Lord, and found out that today was his last day on earth.

Even though I know Christ has redeemed me and the Holy Spirit has sealed me for the day of redemption as a guarantee of my salvation (Ephesians 1:13), I sometimes feel scared when I think about death. I do not doubt the promise of God, but fear plays at the edges of mind nonetheless, and the enemy uses those moments to make me uneasy. We need to continuously go back to God's promises and take heart, for the Lord is with us and has gone before us. When we do this, we can face death with confidence through Christ. After all, Paul reminds us "to live is Christ, and to die is gain" (Philippians 1:21).

So, in order to lead well, we need to prepare for contingencies that will eventually happen and may even take place sooner than expected. We don't do this out of a heart of fear or anxiety, but out of love and concern for our family. Wondering how to do that? Here are a few ways to prepare well.

HAVING A WILL

We do not like to think of our mortality, so talking about the need for a will is usually at the bottom of our lists, discussions, and thoughts. I think each of us would acknowledge the importance of having an up-to-date will, but how many of us actually have one? The reality is that once we die, our possessions, money, and all of our stuff cease to matter to us anymore—but they do matter to our wives and children.

If I die before my wife, I want to make sure that everything goes to her without any opportunity for the courts or another claimant to cause a delay. I want everything to be settled quickly and accurately with my family as the recipients of everything. If my wife and I die at the same time, I do not want the courts to decide who will have custody of our children. I do not want our estate caught up in the legal system while they decide how things should be handled and who should receive any money from it. I bet you want those same things, too.

If you and your wife pass away, who do you want to raise your children? My wife and I found that decision overwhelming. We thought and prayed for a long while before reaching out to some friends and asking if they would be our children's guardians. We wanted to make sure that these guardians had the same faith as us, as well as the same view on education and life.

Whether you have children or not, you will also need to decide who will be the executor of your estate. We went through the same process in this decision.

While you are establishing your will, make sure that all beneficiaries are also up-to-date on life insurance policies and retirement accounts. More details will follow on those, but it is good to confirm the beneficiary information is accurate, and if not, to correct it accordingly.

My wife and I bought a packet of items that had will templates for my will, my wife's will, a living will, power of attorney, and other information.[11] Note that each state has their own rules and regulations for how wills are approved, along with the necessary pieces of the templates, so be sure to fill one out in alignment with your state's requirements. Set aside significant time to fill out the paperwork now, knowing it will make things easier for your family in the future. This may take several "meetings" with your wife. So, set a due date for when you will complete it. I'm not an expert at these matters, but I recommend contacting your lawyer or purchasing a template like we did.

Not sure where to begin?

1. Contact an attorney or purchase a legal packet that fits the needs of your family.
2. Schedule time to fill out the paperwork with your wife.

3. Select an executor of the will (someone who will make sure your will is carried out) and a guardian for your children (if you have children). *Do not take this lightly!*

4. Review/update your will if you already have one.

HAVING LIFE INSURANCE

Insurance is like a shot—it's beneficial but never pleasant. With health insurance, it is a little easier to see it play out because each year my family will have a few annual checkups plus a handful of sick visits. Dental insurance works the same way in my mind—I know I am going to use it this year.

Life insurance is something different. I purchase life insurance to take care of my family in case I die. Let me rephrase that: I purchase life insurance to take care of my family because I *know* I am going to die (just like you and every other person you meet). But I do not know *when* I will die.

Life insurance is essentially a hedge against my life—it is managing risk. Everything in this world and in our lives carries some level of risk, which is okay because risk is not inherently bad. Risk just means a desired outcome is not guaranteed. Some risks can be greater than others or have a greater probability of success or failure than others. Life insurance reduces the risk of financial strain on my family should I die in the next fifteen to twenty years, so I find it worthwhile. I would suggest you consider reducing that risk for your family too.

Life insurance will only pay out if I die within the time-period described by the life insurance policy. If I do not die and the policy expires, then it was money spent with no tangible benefit—so it seems. It is easy to rationalize not purchasing life insurance or just having a token amount because we are going to live until we are old and retire, correct? Yet you and I both know that we can't predict when we will die, and because of this, we want to make sure our wives and children will be provided for after our death. By having life insurance, I reduce the risk of my family struggling financially should I die in the next few years because it guarantees they will have an income even if I am not there. This is another way to love your wife well.

It is much easier and less expensive to acquire life insurance when you are younger, so there is no need to wait. I have had life insurance through the companies I worked for, but when I changed jobs, that insurance was gone. Because of health issues, I also was unable to qualify for life insurance for several years, which was humbling and stressful. Then, when I finally could qualify, it was expensive. I maintained life insurance through my employer until three years ago when I applied and secured a term life policy.

Do you have life insurance? Make sure your policy is updated and that your beneficiaries are current. Don't have life insurance? Look into it today.[12] Remember, this is not about you, it is about your providing for your family after you die.

PLANNING YOUR FUNERAL

If we dared to touch on life insurance, we should also talk a little about funerals. I will not go into too much detail here, but simply suggest that you and your wife have a conversation about what your funeral could look like. As you talk through it, jot down some notes for future reference so that your wife or children do not have to come up with the answers while going through their grief.

These are some questions to answer:

- Casket, cremation, donation?
- Which funeral home would you use?
- Burial? If so, where?
- Viewing or no viewing?
- Funeral at funeral home or church?
- If funeral, are there songs, scripture, or other things to read that you want to include?
- How much will it cost?
- How will you pay for it? (Hopefully through life insurance or savings)

I have a confession to make—my wife and I have not addressed these questions in much detail. We have talked about where we will be buried, specifically which cemetery, but nothing beyond that. I could probably answer most of the questions, but I could not answer all of them. I assume my wife would be the same way. I need to take responsibility and make sure that we have this conversation in the very near future. Are you in the same boat? Do you have this all written out for your wife or are you like me, needing to take action to put this in place?

BRINGING IT TOGETHER

Having a will and life insurance are important, but it is also important that your wife or children can find the documentation in the days that follow your death. My father recently passed away and I was thankful that he had all of the information organized so that my mother could work through the necessary steps with life insurance, pensions, 401k, etc. I saw first-hand the importance and benefit of making sure all of the information is together and in one place.

It does not have to be complicated, in fact it should not be. It needs to be complete, and that just requires a little work and effort on the front end.

1. Start with a list of all of your bank accounts, usernames, and passwords.
2. Next, include any retirement account information, usernames, and passwords.
3. Make a list of life insurance policies along with the insurance company's contact information so that they can be contacted in an efficient and expedient manner.
4. Add a copy of your will, along with any other legal documents.
5. Store all of this information in a safe, file cabinet, or another secure location, like a safety deposit box. Make sure your wife also has access to this information.

Once the information is together, talk through it with your wife. In fact, it is a good idea to talk through it ahead of time and then work through the process together. You can both gather the information, but you as the husband need to take ownership for making sure it is together.

When my wife and I went through this process, we bought a small fireproof safe with a keypad lock to store all of this information, along with birth certificates, social security cards, passports, car titles, and other important documentation. Both of us know the code and can easily access the safe and the contents inside. We gave a copy of our will to the person who would be the executor of our estate, along with instructions on how to access this safe.

Pause for a moment before you continue reading and review the five steps I just mentioned. Which of those have you completed? Which of those do you still need to complete? Write down the steps that you need to complete and show the list to your wife today. When you show her your list, tell her "I love you and I want to make sure that if something happens to me or if I die sooner than expected, all of our information is together and easy to access. Would you help me get this information together today?" If you do this, your willingness to take action will clearly demonstrate your love for her.

That is it. You have settled the information and have prepared your family for when death comes knocking on your door. Does death seem a bit less scary knowing that your family is going to be taken care of?

QUICK HITS FROM THE CHAPTER

- We do not know when we will die, but we can be assured that it will happen someday.

- Having our stuff in order (will, life insurance, funeral) will make it much easier on our families when our deaths occur. They will only have to work through the grieving process, not the grief and stress of not knowing what to do or how to do it.

QUESTIONS FOR REFLECTION

1. Do you have a will, life insurance, and a plan for a funeral?

2. Do you and your wife know where all pertinent information is located should one of you die soon?

3. What one action do you need to take today based on this chapter?

CHAPTER 9

Practice

Time and repetition are two of the best ways that we can lead well at home. Both are needed, but they are distinct in their own ways.

Last night I was cutting branches out of a large tree in our backyard that were hanging down low into our neighbor's yard. The leaves were just starting to come out and I knew that once the limbs had leaves, they would droop almost down to the grass. Cutting them now made the most sense because the limbs would be lighter and easier to trim and carry out to the road.

The only problem with this whole experience was that the limbs were twenty feet above the ground. I was using a pole saw, which if you have never used one before, looks exactly as it sounds—a saw attached to a long pole. If you use a gas or electric pole saw powered by a motor, cutting the limbs is not bad at all, though the saw can be heavy. Unfortunately, I was using one without a motor, which means I manually sawed back and forth on each limb.

I knew the trick was to cut a groove into the tree limb and then stay in the groove as I cut. By doing so, I would cut the same place repeatedly, which takes less effort and goes more quickly. The hard part was starting the groove and then staying there until it became deep enough for the saw to sit easily. While holding the pole saw against a tree limb high in the air, the difficulty of starting the groove and staying there was compounded because I had poor leverage on the saw and the branch. The saw had a tendency to bounce and slide on the branch until I could get it repeatedly in the same groove.

Can you picture me wrangling my pole saw to stay in the groove of the branch twenty feet above my head? Maybe you've been in that predicament before too. After a great deal of effort, I was able to cut the branches and then drag them out of the yard, but it required me to stay focused on the job.

IT TAKES TIME TO DEVELOP THE HABITS

Leading in our homes is a lot like cutting those branches. We start by trying to make a groove and gain some traction, but we can bounce around quite a bit while we try to figure out the best way to do things. It is a lifelong journey of evaluating and adjusting as circumstances change.

Please be encouraged! It takes time to develop these grooves or habits. I have tried many things over the years. Some have worked, many have not. Some went well for a while, then my children got older and the activities were not as effective or they outgrew them. Life changes, so we need to adapt accordingly. The main goal is to establish the habit and practice of looking for ways to engage, teach, spend time, and disciple our wives and children—just like I kept trying to establish a groove in my tree branch.

Practice takes work, but it is not all done in one day. Instead, it is work over time—a little each day, with consistency. I listen to my oldest daughter play piano and it is very different now than when she started a few years ago. The notes and melodies are more complex and the sound is much more advanced. My younger daughter is a vocalist and sounds much different today than before she started vocal lessons. After many hours of practice, singing warmups and range stretching exercises over and over, she is more confident, with clearer sounds and richer tones in her voice. My son recently started playing piano and has progressed far beyond the day when he first sat down and the teacher showed him how to find middle C.

Time, repetition, and consistency are key in any form of success and mastery—from trimming trees to leading our family. Want to learn a language? Spend time on it each day. Learn an instrument? Spend time on it each day. Commit to the doing and then do it. When you do, growth will happen.

SOWING AND REAPING—AGAIN

Much of what we have discussed requires action. I would caution us that if the only thing we change is our actions, we may be missing bigger issues or other areas for growth. **To lead well at home really starts with a heart change that only occurs through Jesus Christ.** I want to point us back to what we mentioned earlier as we evaluated our view of God. If we let the Holy Spirit work in us at the heart level, changing our motives, and helping us to see the beauty and majesty of the Lord, then the actions that will naturally grow from this change will move us toward a desire to lead well. It will not simply be a checklist, but a desire to glorify God through serving our families.

Remember: you get what you plant and reap what you sow.

> For when you were slaves of sin, you were free in regard to righteousness. But what fruit were you getting at that time from the things of which you are now ashamed? For the end of those things is death. But now that you have been set free from sin and have become slaves of God, the fruit you get leads to sanctification and its end, eternal life. For the wages of sin is death, but the free gift of God is eternal life in Christ Jesus (Romans 6:20-23).

Let's plant seeds that produce fruit leading to righteousness in ourselves and our family. May the God of peace be with you as you seek Him and lead your family well.

QUICK HITS FROM THE CHAPTER

- It takes some work to develop a groove when cutting a limb, but once you are in the groove, it goes much easier.

- In the same way, it takes work to get into the patterns and habits of leading well with our families. We need to adjust and work hard to stay in that pattern because when we do, the Lord will bless it.

QUESTIONS FOR REFLECTION

1. What is your number one take-away from this book?
2. On what one thing do you need to spend time, repetition, and consistency?

Vault of Books, Food, and Fun

I've referenced a lot of material in this book, from baking recipes to sword fights, from books to movies. So here's a list compiled into one place as a helpful reference for you as you walk out your calling as husband and father!

Whether you want to try the best brownie recipe on the planet (yes, I am prone to hyperbole!), make swords for you and your child to recreate a pirate battle, or read about Théoden leading his knights into battle on the Pelennor Fields (I get choked up every time I read it), this is the place to start. Pick a story Bible to read with your children and begin leading them each day in Scriptural teaching. Do not limit yourself to this list, however, but use it as a jumping off place for the next step in your journey. Remember, the Lord called you to this, gifting you with your family, *so take heart because He is in control.*

RECIPES

EASY ITALIAN BREAD

This is an easy recipe to begin your bread-making journey. Slice it and eat it warm by itself or slather butter on it. Both ways are delightful. A quick warning though: you need to get a piece quickly because it always disappears swiftly in our home.

Ingredients:

> 2 packages of active dry yeast
> 1 tablespoon sugar
> 2 teaspoons salt
> 1 tablespoon salted butter, melted (unsalted works too)
> 1¾ cups of warm water
> 5 cups of all purpose flour

Ingredients for the egg wash:

> 1 egg white
> 1 tablespoon cold water

Directions:

1. Mix the yeast, sugar, salt, and warm water together.
2. Add the butter and stir.
3. Mix in the first four cups of flour.
4. Slowly add the fifth cup until the dough is soft and able to be kneaded by hand.
5. Place dough on a lightly floured surface and knead for 7-8 minutes. (If dough is sticky, add a little flour, but if it is dry and crumbly, add a little water.)
6. Place the dough in a greased bowl and cover for 30 minutes. (I usually use a towel or foil.)
7. After 30 minutes, remove the dough from the bowl and place on a lightly floured surface. Divide the dough into 2 equal pieces and shape into 2 loaves with your hands. Place the loaves on a baking sheet or into separate loaf pans.
8. Cover with a towel and let the loaves rise for 20 minutes.
9. Preheat the oven to 425°F.

10. Score the top of each loaf with two shallow knife slashes, then bake the bread for 20 minutes. (If you use bread pans, place the pans on the same rack in the oven.)
11. Prepare the egg wash by adding the egg white and tablespoon of water to a small bowl and stir.
12. Remove the bread from the oven and baste the bread with the egg wash. Bake the bread for an additional 5 minutes.
13. Remove the bread from the oven and serve.

BEST BROWNIES ON THE PLANET

These brownies are as easy as a box recipe yet taste three times better. They are my go-to recipe when my children have friends over. These brownies disappear so fast that you would think they were evaporating out of the pan.

Ingredients:

> 2 sticks of butter
> 2 tablespoons of cocoa (I prefer dark cocoa, but regular cocoa works well too)
> 2 cups of sugar
> 1½ cups of all-purpose flour
> 4 eggs

Directions:

1. Preheat the oven to 350°F.
2. Melt butter and place in a large mixing bowl.
3. Add cocoa and sugar to the butter. Mix well.
4. Add eggs and flour. Mix well.
5. Grease a 9" x 13" pan. Add the mixture to the pan and smooth it out.
6. Bake for 30-35 minutes. (You can check if it is done by inserting a toothpick into the brownies. If the toothpick does not have anything on it when you remove it from the pan, they are ready to be taken out of the oven.
7. Let brownies cool somewhat before eating or they will crumble when you remove them from the pan.

BOOKS FOR YOUNG CHILDREN

- *The Gospel Story Bible* by Marty Machowski and A. E. Macha
- *The Jesus Storybook Bible* by Sally Lloyd-Jones and Jago
- *The Big Picture Story Bible* by David Helm and Gail Schoonmaker
- *The Secret of the Hidden Scrolls Books* by M. J. Thomas

BOOKS FOR YOUNGER OR OLDER CHILDREN

- *Amy Carmichael: Rescuer of Precious Gems* by Janet and Geoff Benge (YWAM Publishing)
- *Gladys Aylward: The Adventure of a Lifetime* by Janet and Geoff Benge (YWAM Publishing)
- *William Carey: Obliged to Go* by Janet and Geoff Benge (YWAM Publishing)
- *The Wingfeather Saga, Volumes 1 - 4* by Andrew Peterson
- *The Chronicles of Narnia* by C. S. Lewis

BOOKS FOR OLDER CHILDREN

- *Big Truths for Young Hearts* by Bruce Ware
- *The Lord of the Rings Trilogy* by J. R. R. Tolkien
- *The Screwtape Letters* by C.S. Lewis
- *George Muller: Delighted in God* by Roger Steer
- *The Cost of Discipleship* by Dietrich Bonhoeffer

BOOKS AND BIBLICAL
RESOURCES FOR ADULTS

- ESV Study Bible
- NIV Study Bible
- Apologetics Study Bible (HCSB translation)
- Answers in Genesis www.answersingenesis.org
- Navigators Bible reading plan https://www.navigators.org/wp-content/uploads/2017/04/Discipleship-Journal-Bible-Reading-Plan-9781617479083.pdf

TRUSTED ORGANIZATIONS YOUR
CHILDREN CAN FINANCIALLY SUPPORT

- Compassion International: https://www.compassion.com/
- Samaritan's Purse: https://www.samaritanspurse.org/
- Wycliffe Bible Translators: https://www.wycliffe.org/
- IMB: https://www.imb.org/lottie-moon-christmas-offering/

MOVIES

- Lord of The Rings
- The Chronicles of Narnia
- Pilgrim's Progress
- The Princess Bride

GAMES AND ACTIVITIES

- Go Fish
- Rummy
- Euchre
- Classic board games

HOW TO MAKE POOL NOODLE SWORDS

Items needed:

Pool noodle (each noodle makes two swords)

Tape

Scissors/knife/box cutter/hacksaw

Instructions:

1. Measure the length of the pool noodle and mark the midpoint. Do this in several places around the noodle to give you a rough line to follow when cutting.
2. Carefully cut the noodle along your markings. A hacksaw works well for this, or anything that allows you to make a clean cut.
3. Wrap tape around the end you cut, mimicking the grip or hilt of a sword. The sword hilt can vary in length based on your own design. You can create a shorter hilt for one-handed use or a slightly longer hilt for two-handed use. One variation is to design your hilt on paper and then wrap it around the base of the noodle. Use clear packing tape to secure it to the noodle. Be creative and have fun!

Small Group Discussion Guide

My hope is that these concepts help you examine your heart and turn toward the Lord.

Gather a group of men and intentionally discuss these truths over the next several weeks. Included here are questions for the introduction and each of the nine chapters.

Start by praying and specifically asking the Lord to give you a humble heart for your group discussion. Next, discuss the content of the chapter and answer the questions, making sure to write down action items for you to take home and apply. Finally, pray, asking the Lord to give you the courage to carry out any actions you noted in your discussion.

There is a bonus section of questions based on the Vault of Books, Food, and Fun. Use this as a resource to recap the book together with your group and share ideas with each other.

Keep a notebook with you throughout this study in order to write down your goals and actions. Too often I have made goals, but then did not take action because I could not remember them even an hour later. Remember, plan the work and work the plan.

Together we can be men who love and lead our families well.

INTRODUCTION

1. How has your father's influence affected the way you see your role as a husband or a father?

2. How has the culture affected the way you see your role as a husband or a father?

3. How would you define the biblical role of a husband and father? (You will read more about this in Chapter 1, but this is a good exercise to analyze your current beliefs.)

4. What do you want out of this book? Set at least one goal at the beginning and write it down in your notebook— remember, plan the work and work the plan.

CHAPTER 1: WHERE DO WE START?

1. Do you live your life as a follower of Christ? On what are you basing your answer?

2. Based on how the Bible describes the role of a husband and father, how has your view changed? Was anything new, different, or surprising?

3. How do you already love your wife well? How could you love her more like Christ?

4. What things do you want your children to learn from you (either by observing you or by being taught from you)? What kind of legacy do you want to leave?

5. What action is God asking you to take based on this chapter?

CHAPTER 2: HOW TO START

FRUIT

1. What kind of fruit do you think you are producing? What kind of fruit is your life actually producing? What kind of fruit do you want to produce? How do those compare to one another?

2. As you look at your life today, what kind of seeds are you sowing based on your words and actions, and what kind of fruit are you expecting to grow from those seeds?

TIME

1. How are you growing in relationship to the Lord and spending time with Him?

2. How are you intentionally spending time with your wife and children—not just quality time, but quantity time too?

3. How does your job keep you from being at home or with your family on a consistent basis?

4. If the Lord allows you to reach eighty years of age and you continue to live as you do today, what would be your biggest regret regarding the way you use your time?

MONEY

1. Do you consider yourself a steward of your money or the owner of your money? Why?

2. How can you worship the One who provides instead of the provision?

3. What would your wife and/or children say they want more of and why: stuff or time with you? Elaborate on why they would give that particular answer.

4. What lies has money made you believe about God? Call it out for what it is—a lie—and replace the lie with God's truth.

ATTENTION

1. When you escape, what is the motivation for doing so? To rest? To reflect? To not have to think about life?

2. How has your form of escapism led to relationship struggles with your family?

3. In what ways do you use escapism as a means to avoid responsibility?

4. Consider your forms of escapism. What is it trying to cover up?

CHAPTER 3: PAUSE AND REALIGN

1. What do you struggle with the most: time, money, or attention? Which one would your wife say you struggle with the most?

2. What is one action that your wife would say could help you realign your life to follow Christ better?

3. How are you looking for money to fix your problems and make your life better?

4. What possessions or quest for possessions are keeping you from being generous to God's work?

5. How are you looking at your money and possessions to measure your status compared to those around you? How do you view them as tools given to you by the Lord to use for His work?

6. On what do you think and focus your attention most frequently?

7. How do you center your attention upon the Lord and His purposes?

8. What activities pull you away from the Lord and from your family, and what can you do to change your behavior?

9. From the end of the chapter, how did you answer the three steps to any one of the areas (time, money, attention)?

   - Step 1: Pray to the Lord, asking "Lord, please show me where I need to change?"

   - Step 2: Are you willing to make changes?

   - Step 3: Enact change. Follow through and ask someone to keep you accountable.

CHAPTER 4: LAYING THE GROUNDWORK

1. What does a typical work day look like for you? When do you get up, go to work, come home? How do you usually spend your time in the evenings? Who and what gets your attention?

2. How do you spend time with the Lord? What is your pattern of reading, praying, etc?

3. How can you improve your daily time with the Lord? What changes can you make in your daily/weekly schedule to ensure that you are growing in your faith?

4. Do you have a mentor like Paul? How about a close peer for mutual encouragement like Barnabas? What about someone to mentor like Timothy? Discuss who you are learning from and who you are teaching. Don't forget men who have mentored you in the past (think non-spiritual mentors as well: school teachers, coaches, bosses, etc.).

5. Do you know enough biblically to take the first step in leading a devotional time with your family? What do you have to learn on your own before you can begin doing this?

CHAPTER 5: BE PRESENT WITH YOUR WIFE

1. How do you spend intentional time with your wife?

2. How would your wife like you to spend intentional time with her? What activities do you think your wife would enjoy? If you do not know, sit down with her today and ask.

3. When was the last time you sat down with your wife and listened to her? Do you do this frequently, occasionally, or rarely?

4. When was the last time you said "I love you" to your wife? When was the last time you told her she was beautiful? How can you make this a habit?

5. What is one area or quality you can praise your wife for this week?

6. As a husband, what do you do around the house? Or how could you best serve your wife in your home?

7. Which is harder for you: intentional time with your wife, being emotionally engaged around the house, or verbally encouraging your wife? What one action step can you take today to start changing that pattern?

8. What keeps you from praying with your wife or having a devotional time together? Fear? Busyness? Something else? What one step can you take today to initiate this?

CHAPTER 6: BE INTENTIONAL WITH YOUR CHILDREN

1. How do you spend intentional time with your child(ren)? If you do not have children yet, what is one way you would spend intentional time with them?

2. What is one activity that you could do this week with your children that they would enjoy? Or what activity can you start with your child that can grow into a consistent avenue for connection?

3. When was the last time you said "I love you" to each of your children? When was the last time you said "I am proud of the work and effort you are doing" to each of your children? How can you make this a habit?

4. When you praise your children, what behaviors are you encouraging? Are you concerned more with their success or their effort? What is one area or quality you can praise your children for this week?

5. When you imagine your children's future, what do you envision? Do your desires revolve around successful careers and long life, or do you want each of your children to pursue items of eternal consequence?

6. Are you leading your family toward a faithful relationship with Christ and an investment in a Christ-like church community? If not, what can you change right now to foster that possibility?

CHAPTER 7: BE INTENTIONAL WITH SPIRITUAL MATTERS

1. How frequently do you initiate taking your family to a weekly worship service? Do you have activities that get in the way? Or are your children in so many activities that it prevents you from being able to go to a weekly service? If so, how can you change this?

2. Are you currently in a biblical community (small group, Bible study, etc.)? If not, who can you contact to learn how to become part of one?

3. How are you serving in a local church today? If you are not serving, who can you contact to find out where you can serve?

4. How do you disciple your wife and children? What do you read together? If you're not already doing this, where can you begin?

5. Do you pray with your family excluding meals? If not, pick one day this week to pray with your family for thirty seconds.

6. How do you regularly give money to the work of the Lord? If you do not do this regularly, what one step can you do today to start giving?

7. What spiritual seeds are you sowing in the lives of your wife and children based on your actions today? What kind of harvest will come from those seeds? What changes is the Lord telling you to make?

CHAPTER 8: FINISHING WELL

1. Do you experience fear when the topics of death or eternity come up? What is the source of your fear?

2. How can God's Word help you with your fears about death and eternity?

3. Do you have a will, life insurance, and a plan for a funeral? If not, pick one item and decide how you can start the process of getting it.

4. Do you and your wife know where all pertinent information is located should one of you die? If not, speak with your wife today and select a time within the next week to start collecting this information.

CHAPTER 9: PRACTICE

1. What is your number one take-away from this book?

2. On what one thing do you need to spend time, repetition, and consistency?

3. After reading the introduction, you set one goal for yourself. Did you take a step toward that goal?

4. Is there another man you know who needs to be encouraged and equipped to lead his family well? Reach out to him this week and invite him to read this book with you.

VAULT OF BOOKS, FOOD, AND FUN

1. Just for fun, browse the vault of ideas. Have you read, watched, or tried any of the ideas listed there? Which idea do you want to try first?

2. If you were to create your own vault, what would you recommend to other men, fathers, and husbands?

3. Is there another man you know who would be encouraged by some of the suggestions in this vault? Or by the ideas in your own vault, if you were to create one? Reach out to him this week and share one of the suggestions with him.

Notes

CHAPTER 2

1. *Second-Hand Lions*, directed by Tim McCanlies (2003; Burbank, CA: New Line Home Entertainment, 2004), DVD.

2. Ernest Cline, *Ready Player One* (New York: Broadway Books, 2012).

3. Dolf Zillmann, "Influence of unrestrained access to erotic on adolescents' and young adults' disposition toward sexuality," Journal of Adolescent Health 27 (2), Supplement 1, 2000.

CHAPTER 3

4. Tolkein, J. R. R., "The King of the Golden Hall." In *The Two Towers: Being the Second Part of the Lord of the Rings*. (New York: Ballantin Books, 1982).

5. Tolkein, J. R. R., "The Battle of the Pelennor Fields." In The *Return of the King: Being the Third Part of the Lord of the Rings*. (New York: Ballantin Books, 1965).

CHAPTER 4

6. https://www.navigators.org/wp-content/uploads/2017/04/Discipleship-Journal-Bible-Reading-Plan-9781617479083.pdf

CHAPTER 6

7. Amy Joyce, "Why It's Important to Read Aloud with Your Kids, and How to Make It Count," *Washington Post*, February 16, 2017, https://www.washingtonpost.com/news/

parenting/wp/2017/02/16/why-its-important-to-read-aloud-with-your-kids-and-how-to-make-it-count/

8. Margaret Kristin Merga, "Research Shows the Importance of Parents Reading with Children – Even After Children Can Read," last modified August 27, 2017, https://theconversation.com/research-shows-the-importance-of-parents-reading-with-children-even-after-children-can-read-82756

9. Aaron Earls, "Most Teenagers Drop Out of Church as Young Adults," LifeWay Research, January 15, 2019, https://lifewayresearch.com/2019/01/15/most-teenagers-drop-out-of-church-as-young-adults/

CHAPTER 7

10. Robbie Low, "The Truth About Men and Church," *Touchstone: A Journal of Mere Christianity* 16.5 (June 2003): http://www.touchstonemag.com/archives/article.php?id=16-05-024-v

CHAPTER 8

11. www.uslegalforms.com and www.legalzoom.com are two places to find standard legal packets.

12. I would recommend a term life policy worth ten times your salary with a minimum policy duration longer than the amount of time your children will be in the home.

Acknowledgements

A work like this does not appear out of thin air (even though I wish it did). Along with my work on this endeavor, I would like to thank several people for their suggestions, input, and support.

Thank you Matt W., Matt B., Dane, and Sherman for your encouragement and suggestions to better serve the men in our churches.

Thank you Jana, my wonderful editor, who helped to refine the text and make it clearer to the reader.

Thank you Jenny, for your fabulous design work both inside and outside this volume.

I must thank my three delightful children—Kate, Jill, and Caleb—who remind me each day of the weighty and beautiful charge of fatherhood. You are a gift from the Lord.

Thank you, my beloved wife, Rachel, who not only encouraged me through this writing, but who has encouraged me through our entire marriage. I continually pray that the Lord enables me to be the husband you need me to be.

Lastly, this book only happened because of Jesus Christ and His work in my life. I am an unfinished work taking one step at a time in my sanctification walk, and it is only by His grace, gifting, and strength that anything good comes from my efforts.

About the Author

Eric Rutherford is passionate about equipping the next generation with a biblical worldview and the tools to walk faithfully with Christ. He has been married to his beautiful wife, Rachel, for over twenty years, and they have three delightful children. Eric earned a Master's of Divinity from The Southern Baptist Theological Seminary and is currently an active member of a local church in Murfreesboro, Tennessee. You'll often find Eric and his family reading together or having a movie night at home.

You can read more of Eric's work at www.leadingwellathome.com and www.entrustingthefaith.com.